Discovering Lectio Divina

Bringing Scripture into Ordinary Life

James C. Wilhoit
Evan B. Howard

16pt

Copyright Page from the Original Book

InterVarsity Press
P.O. Box 1400, Downers Grove, IL 60515-1426
World Wide Web: www.ivpress.com
E-mail: email@ivpress.com

©2012 by James C. Wilhoit and Evan B. Howard

All rights reserved. No part of this book may be reproduced in any form without written permission from InterVarsity Press.

InterVarsity Press® is the book-publishing division of InterVarsity Christian Fellowship/USA®, a movement of students and faculty active on campus at hundreds of universities, colleges and schools of nursing in the United States of America, and a member movement of the International Fellowship of Evangelical Students. For information about local and regional activities, write Public Relations Dept., InterVarsity Christian Fellowship/USA, 6400 Schroeder Rd., P.O. Box 7895, Madison, WI 53707-7895, or visit the IVCF website at <www.intervarsity.org>.

Scripture quotations, unless otherwise noted, are from the New Revised Standard Version of the Bible, copyright 1989 by the Division of Christian Education of the National Council of the Churches of Christ in the USA. Used by permission. All rights reserved.

While all stories in this book are true, some names and identifying information in this book have been changed to protect the privacy of the individuals involved.

Design: Cindy Kiple
Images: Bowl of fruit: DEX IMAGE/Getty Images
  Bowl of apples: © Alexey Stiop/iStockphoto
  Orange: © loops 7/iStockphoto

ISBN 978-0-8308-3570-6

Printed in the United States of America ∞

 *InterVarsity Press is committed to protecting the environment and to the responsible use of natural resources. As a member of Green Press Initiative we use recycled paper whenever possible. To learn more about the Green Press Initiative, visit <www.greenpressinitiative.org>.*

Library of Congress Cataloging-in-Publication Data

Wilhoit, Jim.
  Discovering lectio divina: bringing Scripture into ordinary life /
James C. Wilhoit, Evan B. Howard.
    p. cm.
  Includes bibliographical references (p.   ).
  ISBN 978-0-8308-3570-6 (pbk.: alk. paper)
  1. Bible—Hermeneutics. 2. Bible—Reading. 3. Bible—Criticism,
interpretation, etc. I. Howard, Evan B. 1955- II. Title.
  BS476.W49 2012
  248.3—dc23

                                                                          2012009652

| P | 17 | 16 | 15 | 14 | 13 | 12 | 11 | 10 | 9 | 8 | 7 | 6 | 5 | 4 | 3 | 2 | 1 |
| Y | 26 | 25 | 24 | 23 | 22 | 21 | 20 | 19 | 18 | 17 | 16 | 15 | 14 | 13 | 12 |

TABLE OF CONTENTS

PREFACE	iv
1: THIRSTY FOR GOD	1
2: THE DIVINELY SPOKEN SCRIPTURE	21
3: WE WHO LIVE AND READ	42
4: READING	63
5: MEDITATING	83
6: PRAYING	102
7: CONTEMPLATING	125
8: ACTING IN THE MIDST OF THE TRIALS OF LIFE	146
CONCLUSION	161
REFLECTION QUESTIONS AND SUGGESTIONS	166
FOR FURTHER READING	175
NOTES	177
BACK COVER MATERIAL	192

"The authors befriend the Word in such a way that we become better friends of God and more committed members of our faith community. With the help of grace, they convince us that we may be granted as the fruit of such reading a life of active contemplation and contemplative action, moving from *lectio* to *conversio*, that is, the conversion of mind and heart to Christ."

SUSAN MUTO, PH.D., dean, Epiphany Academy of Formative Spirituality and author of *A Practical Guide to Spiritual Reading*

"Evan Howard and Jim Wilhoit not only give us a manual for lectio divina but, more importantly, offer us a practical spirituality of the Word, steeped in the tradition of our ancestors. By reminding us of Martin Luther's understanding of theology as living Scripture in the midst of our difficulties, they challenge us to give birth to the Word we read and pray. This is the fundamental task of Christian spiritual formation."

ALBERT HAASE, O.F.M., author of *Athanasius: The Life of Antony of Egypt, a Paraphrase*

"A most welcome and welcoming book! Wilhoit and Howard, like trustworthy spiritual directors, invite readers to feast in the house of prayer, in which, they tell us, lectio divina resides. As we read, Jesus' disciples, early desert followers of Christ, Reformers, scholars, monks and ordinary Christians join us at the table of God's penetrating, sanctifying Word. Wise and nourishing, *Discovering Lectio Divina* is for all who seek to grow in faith."

SUSAN S. PHILLIPS, PH.D, professor of Christian spirituality, New College Berkeley, and author of *Candlelight: Illuminating the Art of Spiritual Direction*

Formatio books from InterVarsity Press follow the rich tradition of the church in the journey of spiritual formation. These books are not merely about being informed, but about being transformed by Christ and conformed to his image. Formatio stands in InterVarsity Press's evangelical publishing tradition by integrating God's Word with spiritual practice and by prompting readers to move from inward change to outward witness. InterVarsity Press uses the chambered nautilus for Formatio, a symbol of spiritual formation because of its continual spiral journey outward as it moves from its center. We believe that each of us is made with a deep desire to be in God's presence. Formatio books help us to fulfill our deepest desires and to become our true selves in light of God's grace.

PREFACE

In our own lives, we have found the power of Scripture to restore, heal, transform, bring to life, make bearable and bring joy.

In so many ways, this book is a tribute to the people and groups that nurtured us in our faith. While the evangelical Christianity that formed our early faith tended to be less concerned with history, it taught us the basics of lectio divina without ever using that term. We were instructed in how to read, pray, meditate on Scripture, and listen to God in and through it. As we have read more widely, we both return with appreciation to the solid formation we received in those evangelical campus groups and churches.

In this digital age, the claims made about the power of a mere book seem almost preposterous. Yet Christians are asked to believe that God, working through Scripture, can do mighty works. Consider the biblical call to grow in love. How can we do this? A common answer is that we become more adept at loving by loving—by doing acts of love—and there is real wisdom in that response. Yet we know that merely trying to love does not lead to love. Love is a cultivated disposition that flourishes when our minds are trained to honor loving thoughts and our bodies are trained toward loving acts. Lectio divina can help us grow in love by experiencing God's true and healing love as we meditate on his Word and by learning to pay attention to the roots of love—our thoughts.

Lectio divina is part of the curriculum to grow in Christlikeness. Historically it was placed in the center of spiritual formation because of its power to renew us. When Benedict of Nursia established his monasteries, they were intended to be schools of conversion, learning and sanctification. Consequently, lectio divinia was woven into daily life because he understood the power of prayerful reading and meditation on Scripture to shape a life's direction. Similarly, when Martin Luther chose to give brief advice on how to be a good theologian, he chose an approach to Scripture that bears great similarity to that of Benedict.

We are compelled to write this book by a passion for both a broad and a deep approach to Scripture. We are scholars with a strong commitment to the best of biblical scholarship. As such, we are convinced that the transformation of hearts, minds and lives in conformity with the truth of the gospel is best served by using a combination of academic and devotional practices. Our aim here is simply to offer an introduction to the more devotional approach to Scripture.

This is a book written together by two friends, and even though we are separated by half a continent, at this point, it is no longer clear to us who wrote what. We have chosen to use the first person plural, *we*, to reflect this joint writing. From time to time, we will switch to *I* to indicate that a story or contribution is from just one of us, although we won't indicate which one of us as it's generally not relevant.

We are particularly grateful for all the friends who helped us along the way with this book. Many people read all or portions of the manuscript and offered helpful advice: Linda Rozema, Jonathan Kindberg, Bethany Wilson, Neil Wilson, Steve and Kathy Parish, the Norm and Bertha Johnston family, Coky and Janet Hartman, Marti Isler, Sharyn Crayne, Stephanie Noble, Bill Bennett, Penny Paxton, Ruthann Boehler, Larry Day, and Matt and Kristi Andrews. Neil Wilson provided an especially valuable critical review and questions. Similarly, Stephanie Farrier offered a number of valuable copyediting suggestions, while Kathleen Cruse provided help with proofreading and word processing. Amanda Elskens helped with designing the study questions. Additionally, many teaching assistants helped in various ways.

We are also grateful to the staff at InterVarsity Press for all their support. Cindy Bunch has been an admirable guide for us throughout this project. We are grateful to the Scripture Press Foundation for their role in providing Jim with an endowed chair position at Wheaton College, and with this, the encouragement to write about Scripture and life.

Finally, as mentioned above, this book is written by two friends who live at some distance from each other. The two of us met a decade ago in the process of organizing an annual gathering of evangelical scholars in Christian spirituality. Throughout the years, our "scholars gatherings" have not only been supportive environments of academic development as we have evaluated one another's writings, but they have also been precious times of personal sharing as we have opened our hearts to each other. This group has modeled the combination of head and heart that we hope to have communicated in the present volume, and we dedicate this book to them.

1

THIRSTY FOR GOD

We are both fathers. We know one of the unmixed joys of parenting small children: when they come simply to climb up and cuddle in our lap. No toys present, no discipline to administer, no "Daddy, can I?" questions to answer—just father and child being present with each other. It is a delight merely to *be* together without any particular agenda. It is a satisfying pleasure to spend time with a child (or a parent) who is deeply loved and deeply known.

King David portrayed intimacy with God using this parent-child image. He wrote, "But I have calmed and quieted my soul, like a weaned child with its mother; my soul is like the weaned child that is with me" (Ps 131:2). This child comes not to nurse, but simply to enjoy his mother's presence.

This is a book about praying and meditating on Scripture, but it is first and foremost about intimacy with God. Our goal in this book is to introduce a way of reading, praying and meditating on Scripture so that, in the words of Richard of Chichester, "we may see Christ more clearly, love him more dearly, and follow him more nearly."

Soon after the New Testament was completed, Christians were reading their Bibles for joy and transformation, as a way of simply being present with God. This practice of the devotional reading of Scripture was especially popular among those who retreated to the deserts for prayer and renewal. By the fourth century, much of the Christian church accepted the practice of the devotional reading of Scripture. *Lectio divina*—as this practice was named—immersed people in the reading of Scripture, and yet the point was to do the reading in the context of prayer and meditation. The point was to employ the Scriptures as a doorway into transforming intimacy. Our hope is that you might find through this book a way to enter, through the Scriptures, into an ever-transforming intimacy with God.

WE LONG FOR LIVING WATER

We ache. We long for intimacy with God, with ourselves, with others and with the world itself, for we were fashioned for a world vastly different from the one we inhabit. We were made to dwell in Eden: that land where God walked with his people, where labor produced beauty and where harmony was the rhythm of life. On this side of Eden, however, brokenness, injustice, lusts and scarcity leave us with unmet yearnings for a better place. We are born homesick. We feel out of place, and our souls are restless.

The Bible uses the term *thirst* to describe our soul-restlessness: "My soul thirsts for God, for the living God" (Ps 42:2). God desires that our spiritual thirst would propel us to receive his grace. He invites us in Isaiah 55:1-3: "Ho, everyone who thirsts, come to the waters.... Come, buy wine and milk without money and without price ... come to me; listen, so that you may live." This thirst is part of the human condition. Individuals thirst, and they sing songs of longing and yearning. When nations thirst, they have revolutions. Christian psychologist and lecturer Larry Crabb writes, "Beneath the surface of everyone's life, especially the more mature, is an ache that will not go away. It can be ignored, disguised, mislabeled, or submerged by a torrent of activity, but it will not disappear.... An aching soul is evidence not of neurosis or spiritual immaturity, but of reality." Jesus acknowledges this thirst when he tells us, "Blessed are those who hunger and thirst for righteousness, for they will be filled" (Mt 5:6).

The question then is not "Are you thirsty?" but "What are you doing with your thirsts?" What we do with our unsettledness sets the course of our lives. What do we do with our longings, with our really deep unsettledness?

Some of us try to *satiate* them all—right here and now. We feel empty, and we try to end that emptiness by filling it with relationships, with substances, with activities or with experiences. Or we may vaguely sense where these longings are taking us and—not wanting to go there—we *deny* or *distract* ourselves from acknowledging our longings. The strange thing is that we deny our longings with the very means others use to satiate them: innocent busyness, narcissistic entertainment—anything that keeps us from facing the fact that we are not content even in the midst of success and prosperity.

We will go to any length to shelter ourselves from the reality that we are deeply unsettled. We have entire industries in our society devoted to distracting us from the nagging pains of our wounded souls. Sometimes our distractions are dark and malicious. At other times they appear light and benevolent. Sometimes even our Christian habits offer a religiously acceptable distraction from the deeper cries of our heart. We may accumulate inspirational books and conferences notes; we may attend Bible studies; we may share our prayer requests with others; we may participate in endless spiritual discussions. Yet all of these may actually be keeping us from facing our thirsts, our sorrows, our brokenness and our neediness.

Consider the warning of Pascal, the perceptive seventeenth-century mathematician, physicist and inventor, who wrote in his *Pensées* concerning how diversions can be used to numb our senses to our heart's cry.

Sometimes, when I set to thinking about the various activities of men, the dangers and troubles which they face at Court, or in war, giving rise to so many quarrels and passions, daring and often wicked enterprises and so on, I have often said that the sole cause of man's unhappiness is that he does not know how to stay quietly in his room.

Pascal saw that so many of his peers fled from facing the longings of their hearts. Most did this through diversions. Many of the diversions were trivial, some noble and others quite horrific; regardless, the unwillingness to "stay quietly in [our] room" is deeply seated. Because of this tendency toward distraction, we can see why solitude has long been regarded as an important spiritual discipline. Solitude forces us to sit with ourselves and acknowledge our thirst.

The emphasis in Scripture is on *satisfying* our thirst rather than trying to satiate it or deny it. Jesus had the audacity to say that he could quench the thirst of our souls. He told the woman at the well, "But those who drink the water I give will never be thirsty again. It becomes a fresh, bubbling spring within them, giving them eternal life" (Jn 4:14 NLT). The living water is offered by Christ and provided by the Spirit (see Jn 7:37-39).

Even in the end of the end, when all has been set right, a spiritual thirst persists. Yet people understand the nature of their longing for God, and the water to satisfy it is more readily at hand:

> The Lamb at the center of the throne will be their shepherd, and he will guide them to springs of the water of life. (Rev 7:17)
>
> To the thirsty I will give water as a gift from the spring of the water of life. (Rev 21:6)
>
> The angel showed me the river of the water of life, bright as crystal, flowing from the throne of God and of the Lamb. (Rev 22:1)
>
> And let everyone who is thirsty come. Let anyone who wishes take the water of life as a gift. (Rev 22:17)

It is not surprising that we thirst. Thirst is natural. The question is what we do with our thirst. Do we try to satiate it? Do we deny it or distract ourselves from acknowledging it? Or do we turn to God to satisfy our thirst?

In this book, we offer to you a time-honored way of letting Scripture take you before God, where the thirsts of your soul can be met. Both of us know the experience of coming before God in Scripture just to enjoy the presence of his company. Both of us have—over many years—used Scripture as a means of facilitating leisurely intimacy with God. We have come to Scripture with our thirsts and have found them satisfied. Even when they have remained, the thirsts are often transformed, and they always draw us to God.

THE INVITATION TO MEDITATE

Over the centuries Christians have turned to the psalms as a favorite place for guidance on praying and meditating. The book of Psalms is a collection of spiritual poems and lyrics written over several centuries by many authors and assembled with care and purpose. What we know as Psalm 1 was placed at the beginning of this collection to serve as a prologue. The earliest Christian commentators affirm this, with Jerome (c. 347-420) describing Psalm 1 as a preface inspired by the Holy Spirit to provide a guide to the Psalter. Psalm 1 invites us to meditate on the psalms that follow.

When seen as an introduction, the first psalm alerts us that the psalter shows us two ways of living—one way that results in human flourishing and another that leads to withering. Walking in the way of flourishing involves a two-fold process: saying no to the lures of destructive counsel—"Do not follow the advice of the wicked" (Ps 1:1)—and saying yes to the counsel offered in Scripture by embracing and treasuring it—"Their delight is in the law of the LORD, and on his law they meditate day and night" (Ps 1:2).

Those who meditate "are like trees planted by streams of water" (Ps 1:3). These trees are most likely date palms, which are a source of food and vital materials. The "streams of water" a rare occurrence in ancient Israel, describe irrigation canals that are constantly full. What this first psalm offers is a radical way of addressing our deep thirst. We refuse to follow the advice of the wicked: to deny or to satiate our thirst. Instead we simply plant ourselves near the law of the Lord to allow the deep, thirsty parts of our lives to be habitually exposed to it. Psalm 1 tells us to focus on putting down deep roots that can draw the spiritual nourishment our souls need. One way of putting down those deep roots is meditating on Scripture. How do we deal with our deepest thirst? We plant ourselves by the streams of living water. We meditate on Scripture. And what happens? "Their leaves do not wither. In all they do, they prosper" (Ps 1:3).

In this book we invite you into a practice called lectio divina. While this Latin phrase means "divine lesson" *(lectio* eventually comes to mean "reading," but at first it referred to the actual text), it describes a practice of prayerful reading of Scripture, where the Word comes to saturate our minds and our lives. It has been rightly called "a methodless method." The practice seemingly springs forth spontaneously from a life committed to Scripture, prayer and the imitation of Christ. Through the centuries, many wise Christians have provided guidance on how to cultivate this practice.

Benedict of Nursia (480-547) was one of the earliest to use the phrase "lectio divina." To guide his monastic community, he developed a set of guidelines for their life together, known today as the Rule of Saint Benedict. In the Rule, he built into the very fabric of community life an emphasis on Scripture and prayer. Concerned that "idleness is the enemy of the soul," he stipulated that "the brothers should have specified periods for manual labor as well as for prayerful reading."

Benedict built into their rhythm of life the time for prayerful focus on Scripture. At the same time, Benedictine culture sought to treat reading, meditating, praying, copying, listening to, memorizing, analyzing, interpreting, studying and applying Scripture as one inseparable whole. Nevertheless, over time Christians began to emphasize particular components of this practice: reading *(lectio)*, meditating *(meditatio)*, praying *(oratio)* and contemplating *(contemplatio)*.

While lectio divina—with each of its various components—has been taught as a kind of technical spiritual skill, many many people practice lectio without ever being aware of the phrase or any of the various models of the practice that have been proposed over the centuries. Our aim in this book is to introduce lectio divina for what we feel it is: a natural process by which sincere Christians devotionally read their Bibles.

Protestant Reformer Martin Luther (1483-1546) was asked to write an introduction to the Wittenberg edition of his works. He was reticent to have all his works published, hoping that the Reformation would lead to an increase in the study of Scripture itself rather than the multiplication of scholars' tomes. But because they were being published and he was invited to write the introduction, Luther used the opportunity to teach his understanding of a "correct way of studying theology." He pointed specifically to Psalm 119 as a model of the process. He stated, "There you will find three rules, amply presented throughout the whole Psalm. They are *Oratio, Meditatio, Tentatio.*" Our prayer for the help of the Spirit *(oratio)*, our repetitive reflection on the words of Scripture *(meditatio)* and our sincere pursuit of God in the midst of the trials of life *(tentatio)* are the ways to truth. As Luther wrote, "If you study hard in accord with his [David's] example, ... then do not be afraid to hope that you have begun to become a real theologian."

> Lectio divina, which literally means divine reading, is a process of formational reading that emphasizes a slow dwelling with the text. We can speak of it as containing four ways of being with the text. These are not steps; though they form a logical order, they may happen in any order or simultaneously. Often Latin titles are used to label these four ways.

- *Lectio.* This describes a slow and careful reading of the text and includes much of what we would label as study.
- *Meditatio.* The meditation called for is meditation on the Scripture being read. It may involve savoring, repeating, thinking about or digesting the words so that they become personally meaningful and nourish us spiritually.
- *Oratio.* Here we pray the Scripture. We pray to God for understanding. We pray back to God the promises found, we use this reading to cry out to God or we listen for his voice in what we read.
- *Contemplatio.* We rest in God's presence through the Scripture.

As we shall see, other titles (for example, *tentatio,* struggle; *operatio,* action) have also been used.

Lectio divina is a "both/and" way of being with the text. We read carefully and analytically, but we also savor its beauty and its personal message. We sit quietly before God through the path prepared by reading, but we cry out in joy or anguish as we bring together our life, the world and the text. We zealously chew and ponder the text, and we happily bathe in it.

Like Benedict, Luther saw the value of a meditative reading of Scripture. Indeed, he saw it as a correct way of studying theology. And like the Benedictines, Luther identified a set of related components within this process (prayer, meditation, struggle). In our studies we have found it helpful to explore both Lutheran and Benedictine components in dialogue. Hence, in this book we simply reintroduce a practice that has been common to the whole of the Christian church: the meditative reading of Scripture employed to facilitate a transformative intimacy with God.

THE SWEETNESS AND BITTERNESS OF SCRIPTURE

Imagine a man driving home for Thanksgiving. The wipers streak the windshield and the wind howls as he makes the five-hour drive. The drive is hard, but he knows it is worth it to be home for the holiday. He is drawn by the memories, times of care and closeness; his memories of past Thanksgivings and hopes buoy him as he drives alone through the pouring rain. Yet there are also dark memories—angry words, some his own, spoken the last time they were all together.

As he gets closer, the mix of competing emotions inside becomes harder to ignore. He parks a few doors down from the house to sort out what he is feeling. He calls on all the courage he can, thinking about how his dad would have wanted them to all get along. But he just can't go in. He longs to savor the familiar foods, to hear the stories of when they were all together. He yearns for their laughter. But the longer he waits, the more he fears that only condemnation awaits him.

As he sits, he realizes how cold he is. He watches the house lights. *Do they really miss me?* He turns on the car, but can't drive away. Part of him just wants more than anything to be home. He will wait just a bit longer. *Maybe they'll look for me.*

The man in our story was both drawn toward and repelled by the same thing. This combination of attraction along with fear and revulsion is such a common human experience that the father of social psychology, Kurt Lewin, dubbed it the approach-avoidance conflict. We want to spend the evening with friends (approach), but are hesitant about getting home late on the night before an important early meeting (avoidance). Our lives are filled with these double-bind situations, like the love of spicy food, which is tempered by the certain knowledge that we'll pay for our indulgence later. We may love the look of a coat, but hesitate because of the cost. Whether we call them trade-offs, pluses and minuses, pros and cons, or relational pulls and pushes, we all have firsthand experience in the tug of war of basic needs.

Consider how the book of Revelation describes John's experience of deeply encountering Scripture: "So I went to the angel and told him to give me the little scroll; and he said to me, 'Take it, and eat; it will be bitter to your stomach, but sweet as honey in your mouth.' So I took the little scroll from the hand of the angel and ate it; it was sweet as honey in my mouth, but when I had eaten it, my stomach was made bitter" (Rev 10:9-10).

Let's face it. We come to Scripture with our thirst, but sometimes when we drink, it doesn't taste so sweet. Consequently, many of us experience an approach-avoidance conflict toward Scripture. We are drawn to it (we look to it for guidance, for solace, for a place to meet God), and yet we shy away from it (we may have memories of how it was used in an authoritarian way, or we may feel uncomfortable with some of its teachings). We are pulled by its lure and by the great tradition that honors it, but our experience leaves us conflicted at times. At these times, our approach-avoidance conflict often resolves itself by finding a place where our attraction and our avoidance are comfortably balanced—we limit our reading to a rehearsal of a favorite passage or to a glance at the text from this week's liturgy.

The scroll in Revelation is given to John by Christ, here pictured as an angel. This book contains the message of redemption, and like a passport, it marks our identification with Christ. Two qualities of this book should be noted. First, it is to be eaten—taken into our hearts. Centuries earlier, Ezekiel was exhorted to "eat this scroll" (Ezek 3:3) so that he would "get all these words that I'm giving you inside you. Listen to them obediently. Make them your own" (Ezek 3:10 *The Message*). This book is not just to be handled, placed on a shelf or merely read, but internalized.

Second, it is a book that is both sweet and bitter. The apostle John found sweetness in its comforting words of God's reign, and its bitterness came through the disturbing message of judgment. The prospect of eating honey is far more appealing than that of eating something that upsets the stomach. What is said of this symbolic scroll is also true of the Bible—a book to be internalized and yet a book that disturbs.

We come to the Bible as a means of quenching our thirst for God, and rightly so. Yet we find the Bible to be a mix of both alluring sweetness and soul-confusing bitterness. We experience its sweetness, but we are also confused by its strangeness, and sometimes reading it leaves a bitter taste.

This response is not as odd as it may seem. The Bible is a book with an intimate message, and intimacy raises fear. One man, who loved the Scripture and translated them, wrote that he "who has closely studied these letters for several years is struck by ... their surprising vitality.... He is continually struck by the living quality of the material on which he is working ... again and again the writer felt rather like an electrician rewiring ancient house without being able to 'turn the mains off'" The power he found was both invigorating and scary.

Think of the last time you opened the Bible. Why did you open it? We open the Bible for a number of reasons. We hear it read in church gatherings. We study it for truth and guidance. We use it for God's glory and for self-defense. It comforts the challenged and challenges the comfortable. The Bible is not all sweetness, but what John described as the bitter is also needed. We are nourished by sweet and bitter alike. In this bent and hurting world, it is actually good to know that the Bible can offer both a sweet and a bitter word. And if we learn to surrender to God's love as we read, the intimacy we find allows us to receive the bitter with the sweet.

WE HOPE FOR TRANS-FORMATION

The word we ingest in lectio divina is not only a *nourishing* word, but also a *transforming* word. This, too, is actually a quenching of our thirst, for we thirst not only for intimacy, but also for the transformation of personal and community life that flows from such intimacy. More specifically, with regard to the reading of Scripture, we long to have our association with "sacred text" lead to a more "sacred life."

Consequently, it will be helpful to consider briefly the character of Christian spiritual formation, for lectio divina is a *formational* reading of the text. As human beings, we are being formed every day of our lives. Our genetic programming began to form us before we were born. Our parents formed us from the moment of our birth, by their presence or by their absence. Our culture forms us, making a Chinese life different from a Canadian life. Furthermore, we are all formed *spiritually* in the course of life. Our experiences of life influence us toward belief in God or away from faith.

Christian spiritual formation is the process by which followers of Jesus become conformed to Christ, especially with regard to our maturity and calling. It is *"Spiritual"* formation: the Spirit of Christ is the primary former. Yet it is also intentional: we who are formed take an active role in this process. Christian spiritual formation is communal: our formation is not simply a matter of me and God, but rather involves others who shape me and who grow with me. And it has its means and end in the imitation of Christ: formation is a process of trying to do what Jesus did, think like Jesus thought, feel like Jesus felt, in order to become more like Jesus in every area and every moment of our lives.

One means by which our formation in Christ is fostered is the practice of a meditative reading of Scripture. Once again, we turn to the psalms. Read Psalm 19:7-10:

The law of the LORD is perfect,

reviving the soul;
the decrees of the LORD are sure,
making wise the simple;
the precepts of the LORD are right,
rejoicing the heart;
the commandment of the LORD is clear,
enlightening the eyes;
the fear of the LORD is pure,
enduring forever;
the ordinances of the LORD are true
and righteous altogether.
More to be desired are they than gold,
even much fine gold;
sweeter also than honey,
and the drippings of the honeycomb.

The psalmist poetically links words for Scripture (law, decrees, precepts and so on) with descriptions of their virtues (perfect, sure, right and so on) and of their functions (reviving the soul, making wise, rejoicing and so on). The section closes with two powerful images of their precious value (gold and honey).

Like the first psalm, Psalm 19 paints a picture of Scripture as a source of flourishing. Through the law, our soul is revived. Through the Lord's precepts, our heart rejoices. Through God's commandment, our eyes are enlightened. Yet in Psalm 19, this is not merely a picture of *nourishment,* but also a description of *transformation.* The law of God functions not merely to satisfy our thirsts, but also to transform them from the inside out. Where do we go for the transformation we desire? We meditate on Scripture.

Imagine how this works. You attend a Bible study; a few friends sitting around a passage of Scripture, wrestling together with a few hard questions. As you give the passage some time to soak in, an idea is born. Your perspective enlarges. A belief emerges. "I hadn't seen things that way before," you say. Your worldview is changed.

Or perhaps you are alone in your place of quiet, reading a story from the Gospels, picturing in your mind what it must have been like to be there with Jesus. And as you are there with Jesus, something "clicks." You realize—deep inside—that Jesus loves purely, beautifully; that Christ loves *you* with that same love here and now. And with tears in your eyes, you experience the healing love of God.

Or perhaps you are struggling with some misdirected thirst (say, for example, an obsession with clothing), and after months of reading and reflecting on Proverbs and Ecclesiastes, you see a commercial for the latest fashions and notice that the impulse to buy is not quite so strong. Meditation, in time, leads to transformation.

The Spirit of God *fills* us, satisfying our deep thirst for More. The Spirit *teaches* us, revealing to us the truth of God (see Ps 119). The Spirit also *forms* us, remaking our feelings, molding our habits, guiding our relationships, comforting us when we are disturbed and disturbing us when we are too comfortable. Indeed, any and every aspect of life can be open to the Spirit's transforming work. And as with the Spirit's thirst-filling work, we facilitate it by giving time to the Spirit-inspired Scriptures—divine reading.

In the rest of this book we will share wisdom we have gleaned about the practice of lectio divina—how to saturate our lives with prayer and Scripture as we live with hands open to receive from God, ready to cry out for the needs of the world and of those we face daily. In chapter two, we will look at the divine side of things, particularly at Scripture as the divinely spoken word of God. Just what *is* Scripture, and how does it relate to our relationship with God? Then, in chapter three, we will introduce you to the human side of divine reading—how the human person contributes to and receives from devotional reading.

Chapters four through eight lead you through five different aspects of this prayerful lifestyle with Scripture: reading, meditating, praying, contemplating and acting in the midst of the trials of life. We see these aspects not as a necessary sequential progression for divine reading or life, but rather simply as five different "things we do" that shape our intimate presence with God through the Scriptures.

2

THE DIVINELY SPOKEN SCRIPTURE

My friend's grandfather emigrated from Europe in the late nineteenth century. He arrived broke in New York City and set out to make his way to his relatives' homestead in the Midwest. He took the train as far as his limited money would take him and decided to walk the remaining distance. It was early spring, and he found farm work here and there, which he could do in exchange for food and lodging. He also learned early on that he could sleep in churches. He was not particularly religious, but a hard church pew was better than a barn and a rude awaking by an angry farmer. The churches all had Bibles, and he began to read them. He struggled at first with this foreign tongue. Drawn along by curiosity and a desire to learn English, he read every night he was in a church.

As the summer wore on, he found that the reading had done a great work in his heart. As he tells it, he left New York with no interest in religion, but after months of reading the Bible every night, he arrived at the family homestead a committed follower of Christ. Through reading the Scriptures, God had acted to renew this man's heart and implant in him new virtues and commitments. "The old life is gone. A new life has begun!" (2 Cor 5:17 NLT).

Consider the promises of the Psalms. Psalm 1: the water is the law of God; the tree is our life. Meditation is the activity through which the water flows from the river to nourish the tree. The person who meditates on God's word, like the tree nourished by the waters of a nearby river, will prosper. Psalm 119: the commandments of God make us wiser than our teachers. Psalm 19: the Lord's words revive our soul, bring stability to our lives and allow us to put off the dominant life pattern of the world. As in these psalms, Joshua associated flourishing with meditation, urging that "this book of the law shall not depart out of your mouth; you shall meditate on it day and night, so that you may be careful to act in accordance with all that is written in it. For then you shall make your way prosperous, and then you shall be successful" (Josh 1:8).

The promises are clear. Meditation is the path to a flourishing life—the way to the life you truly desire. Meditate on the "word of life" (Phil 2:16) and acting in accordance with it will follow naturally. Do you want to understand and communicate the truth of the Christian faith? Biblical meditation is a path to wisdom, to flourishing, to enlightening, and it is the central piece of lectio divina. In lectio divina, two elements join: water and tree; Scripture and soul; divine and human. Divine reading. In this chapter, we will speak about the divinely spoken Scripture. In the next we will turn our attention to we who read.

Both experience and the Scriptures themselves teach us that the Bible is a powerful book, a life-changing book. But simply *because* the Bible is such a powerful book, it has been powerfully misused to cause great harm on earth.
- Bible passages have been quoted by men to justify the abuse of their wives and children.
- Bible teachings have been distorted by politicians to justify the pollution of the earth.
- Bible stories have been retold by church leaders to justify the hatred of other peoples.

It is so easy to acknowledge (rightly) the divine origin and authority of Scripture only to associate (wrongly) our own private agendas with some part of it. The Pharisees were masters of the art of employing particular texts and teachings to their own advantage and under the claim of the divine power and authority of Scripture. Often, in this kind of misuse, the divine character of Scripture is emphasized to the neglect of the human contexts within which the text should be properly understood. Jesus had some harsh words to say about this misuse of Scripture.

Others, seeing how Scripture has been abused through the centuries, respond by rejecting the divine character of Scripture entirely. They see the Bible merely as a human record of the development of the Judeo-Christian people, a story of religion just as we might find in any other religious history. They see the Bible as a book of good advice, perhaps, but they don't acknowledge the uniquely divine power and authority of the Bible.

Pontius Pilate, the Roman governor of Judea, was an example of this misunderstanding. Jesus, in his trial before Pilate, claimed to testify to the truth. Pilate asked him, "What is truth?" He could not understand Jesus' absolutism. And in the end, he sentenced Jesus to death as a challenge to the Roman emperor. The approach of Pilate to Jesus is the approach of many people to the Scriptures today.

So, just what is Scripture? How are we as readers to approach such a text? As we can see, these are no minor issues. And these are the questions explored in this chapter. We will begin by considering a few concepts used to describe the Bible. This will lead us into reflections on the notion of the Bible as "God's Love Letter" and as *divinely* spoken Scripture. We will look at the human side of Scripture—a record of human relationship with God. We will conclude by seeing something of the Scripture's function as an invitation to relationship with God.

GOD'S WORD IN HUMAN SPEECH

Two common terms used to describe the character of Scripture are *revelation* and *inspiration*. The Bible is first a revelation from God. What this means is that God has chosen to reveal himself to us through this book, just like we might choose to let you know something about us by writing our autobiographies. Whereas the created order reveals something about the Creator in a more general way, Scripture manifests God's life and will in a more specific, verbal way. It is God's *Word*.

This makes the Bible a very special book (unlike our autobiographies), for it is also a specific, verbal revelation of *God*. Monk and author Thomas Merton (1915-1968) wrote, "The Bible claims to contain a message which will not merely instruct you, not merely inform you about the distant past, not merely teach you certain ethical principles, or map out a satisfying hypothesis to explain your place in the universe and give your life meaning—much more than that, the Bible claims to be: The Word of God." The Creator and Redeemer of the universe speaks to us through this book. Consequently, what it says carries a lot of weight.

Yet the Christian Scriptures are a different kind of revelation from an autobiography in another way. Whereas we might sit down and write our story, God did not author the Scriptures in this manner. Various people, over a long period, wrote the Bible. And yet we call it *God's Word*. "Your word is a lamp to my feet and a light to my path" (Ps 119:105). So whose word is it: "God's or other people's? This is where we must speak of inspiration" Inspiration is the process whereby "men and women moved by the Holy Spirit spoke from God" (2 Pet 1:21).

Think about it. We could tell an administrative assistant what to say—word for word. He could type it up, thereby writing our "word." This is called dictation, and perhaps only a small portion of the Bible was dictated by God to the authors (such as the Ten Commandments, written on tablets of stone by the finger of God). We could have a technical writer write our piece, providing guidance about the nature of the content and yet allowing the personality and background of the writer to show through in the final work. This more closely resembles what we call inspiration.

But the inspiration of Scripture—as the expression of *God*—is special, just as the revelation of the Scripture as God's word is special. The Spirit of God, being divine, oversees this inspiration process such that the words and expression of Scripture are *both* naturally and authentically the words of the different writers *and* just what God wants to say. We listen *through* the words of people *to* the voice of God.

And because it is the word of *God*, we must listen to these human words with profound care.

As Scottish mathematician, economist, and church leader Thomas Chalmers (1780-1847) put it, "If the New Testament be a message from God, it behooves us to make an entire and unconditional surrender of our minds, to all the duty and to all the information which it sets before us." Because the Scriptures are a revelation from God through human words to us, we must begin to open the Scriptures by opening ourselves to hear God. And what God brings us through this book is a message of love.

GOD'S LOVE LETTER

Just as I would reveal something of myself through a work of art, so God reveals something of himself through nature. Just as I might reveal my character through a personal visit, so Jesus reveals the character of God. And just as a letter might reveal the heart of the sender, so Scripture is a window into the heart of God. Indeed, Scripture is sometimes called a "love letter" from God. Danish philosopher Søren Kierkegaard (1813-1855) said of God's revealing Scripture, "So willing is he, infinite love, so willing to become involved with a person that he has written love letters to us in his word, has proposed to us and said: come, come..." What a delightful thought to imagine the Bible as a love letter, and an invitation to love, written directly from God to me!

Yet the Bible does not always read like a love letter. We open to the books of Kings and find stories of intrigue and massacre. We open to the book of Psalms and hear the psalmist cry, "How long, O Lord? Will you forget me forever?" (Ps 13:1). We open to the Gospels and hear Jesus calling other religious leaders a "brood of vipers" (Mt 12:34). It does not always sound very loving. And it does not always seem to be written to *me*. Those commandments in Numbers regarding gleaning seem to have little reference to contemporary urban life. Paul's letters were written to churches and pastors, not ordinary people like me. Besides, it does not seem very intimate to think of every human being in the world, throughout time, reading the Bible as his or her own personal love letter.

Let's suppose I wanted to write my love letter not merely to an individual but to a group of people, a group of people in which you were included. I might speak of how I have experienced you all and how I long to be near each and all of you. I might speak of my desire that you would live in a way that pleases me. How would you read that letter? Certainly you would not assume that each statement was meant for you personally. Different members of the group experience different circumstances, and you would realize that this letter reflected the breadth of the experiences of the receivers.

But at the same time, you would be sensitive to the fact that this letter *is* written to you: both as part of the group generally and in some measure to you personally. You would relish those tender phrases written to the group (and to you). You would be especially attentive to the statements that might have direct reference to you. Indeed, if you were to read the same letter again later, you might encounter a phrase that was originally meant for another, yet now is especially relevant to you. And since it expresses the concerns of your beloved, you take it to heart.

But what if I thought this group in which you were included might not really understand my love simply by hearing a few intimate expressions? Perhaps the best way of revealing my love would be to tell a story, a story of my own involvement in the group's life? And what if this story spoke of the group's life over a long period, in much of which you were not even present? And what if this story included tales of violence and confusion? In this form of expression, the writing might not even look like a letter.

Nevertheless, while you might be confused by a few pieces, you would still understand the point. You would see yourself as part of it and be touched by those expressions of love that were felt by the group even when you were not around. You might notice statements made or desires expressed at one distant point of this story that are especially relevant for you here and now. You would apply them to your life, since they reveal to you some aspect of the character of your beloved. And this would be proper, for my *intention* was that you would see yourself as part of this group. Thus, through this story—even when it does not look like a letter—you would understand the communication of love that was being expressed through it.

And consider this: What if this story of my love encompassed such a long period that it was best told from the mouths of the many people who experienced it? Indeed, what if this was a millennia-long story? And what if the story was best told with illustrations from other literature of this or that period that also demonstrated my love for this group (in which you were included)? Now my "love letter" might look more like a collection of stories, poems, legal documents, prophetic proclamations and all kinds of bits and pieces of writing.

On the one hand, these various writings would, in their telling of my encounters with the group, *bear witness* to my love. They would speak of the ways that I revealed my love to the group at that point in time. Yet, insofar as I was actively involved in the assembly of these various writings into a single coherent collection (inspiration), the result would not simply be a collection of witnesses to my revelation but would be *revelation itself*, a purposeful expression of my love for this group.

Again, you would understand. True, you might have difficulties trying to reconcile this legal statement with that poetic phrase, but you would be reading this document in the right frame of mind. You would learn to see this document—the expression of love from a lover to a beloved—as a magnificent and vast (albeit complicated), interconnected letter of love. By this time, you might realize that the riches of such a love letter may take a lifetime (or more) to grasp.

Finally, what if I happened to slip nearby you as you read this long letter? What if I whispered a hint here and there regarding what was meant by this or that phrase? What if I whispered what this or that phrase might mean for *you*? How would you read this letter if you knew and expected this "slipping nearby" to take place, although you knew not when? Reading in this way could get a little exciting, or perhaps even a bit scary, but being able to consult with the author could also give you confidence.

This is how we are to understand Christian Scripture. It is a written document of intentional communication from one living person (God *is* personal) to another. Paul proclaimed, "All scripture is inspired by God" (2 Tim 3:16). This word *inspired* literally means "God breathed." Just as God breathed life into humankind through the Spirit in Genesis 2, so God, through the Spirit inspires/breathes himself to humankind through the Scriptures. This is why Christians see the

Bible as a living book. "Indeed, the word of God is living and active, sharper than any two-edged sword, piercing until it divides soul from spirit, joints from marrow; it is able to judge the thoughts and intentions of the heart" (Heb 4:12). This collection of narratives, poems and epistles is an intentional expression of God's love and his invitation into love. True, there may be portions of this expression that appear confusing or even offensive (sweet and bitter). The love language of Scripture can be hard to see sometimes. Even Peter expressed his exasperation when he mentioned, regarding Paul's writing, "There are some things in them hard to understand" (2 Pet 3:16).

While we are wise to explore what is involved in the ambiguities of this book—any lover would pursue the heart of the beloved in his or her writings—still we do not lose faith when faced with its complexities. Rather, we read the text with an ear for the Composer who not only is revealed in the text, but whose Spirit whispers to us as we read, reminding us of the heart of Christ (see Jn 14:26). Theologians call this whispering "illumination," and we will explore illumination more in the chapters ahead.

THE DIVINELY SPOKEN SCRIPTURE

God in his love has chosen to reveal himself. We understand God to be self-sufficient and not in need of our gifts and service. God is not "served by human hands, as though he needed anything, since he himself gives to all mortals life and breath and all things" (Acts 17:25). He has chosen to speak to us because he desires to be in relationship with us—he desires to make friends with us.

We describe people who reveal something of themselves to us as "open." *Open* captures an important dimension of what we call revelation. The term *revelation* is derived from the Latin word *revelatio*, and it means "uncovering." Something that was hidden has been opened or uncovered for us to see. We are unable to know God directly through our observations—unless he makes the first move, and he has done just that.

God's most dramatic act of revelation was that of his Son, the Word made flesh: "but in these last days he has spoken to us by his Son" (Heb 1:2 TNIV). In this event God came and pitched his tent among us—that is the literal meaning of "dwelt among us" (Jn 1:14 NASB). He showed his character and showed his values through his life so that Jesus could say, "Whoever has seen me has seen the Father" (Jn

14:9). In God becoming flesh, we have full disclosure of God. But what about those of us who live millennia after Jesus' early life: how do we receive this revelation? We receive it through the Bible, which not only reports what Jesus said and did, but also provides the story of why and how Christ came to live among us.

When we pick up the Bible, we pick up a unique book that is the result of a double authorship. It is both fully the Word of God and the word of its human authors, nothing other than "the Word of God through the words of human being," as John Stott described it. The text of the Bible describes itself both as the speech of God and as a book with genuine human authors through whom "God announced long ago through his holy prophets" (Acts 3:21). The writing of this extraordinary book would have looked quite ordinary when it was composed: "So Jeremiah called in Baruch son of Neriah. Jeremiah dictated and Baruch wrote down on a scroll everything that GOD had said to him" (Jer 36:4 *The Message*).

Before we even begin reading a book, we make assumptions about how to approach it. We pick up a dictionary with a different intent than we pick up a novel by a favorite author. This is overwhelmingly true of our approach to the sacred text of the Bible. We are better readers and obeyers of the Bible when we come to it in a way that is different from the way we approach other books. Yet, since it has human authors who were quite artistic in their compositions, we do well to read the Bible as human literature, sensitive to the literary conventions or "rules" specific to each type of literature within it. Since so much of it is addressed to specific situations, we read it best when we have a grasp of what is going on in the stories. And since it is a book filled with great ideas, we should read it with an appreciation for the complexity and richness of the thought expressed.

But there is more. The Scriptures are not just a place where we read about God—the Scriptures are "living and active." They are a place where we receive from God. Someone may casually speak of "getting a blessing" from reading the Bible, and that is absolutely right. God acts toward us when we read his word—that is one way that reading the Bible is radically different from reading any other book.

As we read the Bible, we find instructions, moral teachings, images and history. In and through these different writings, we learn of God's active involvement in human affairs. We can perceive God acting with relationship to *us* even as we read the writings of Scripture. We not only read about God's blessings, we receive blessing; we do not just overhear the Father telling Jesus that he is the beloved of God, we also hear those words about Jesus spoken to us.

A RECORD OF HUMAN RELATIONSHIP WITH GOD

When we imagine Scripture as a love letter, we view the text from the point of view of the *divine sender*. From this point of view, our almighty, heavenly Lover assembles, from human history, a collage of writings sufficient to communicate his love, and through them he invites us to respond. There are other ways, however, of viewing Scripture. How might we picture Scripture from the point of view of the *human authors* of the various books?

One way might be to see the texts of Scripture as records of human relationship with God. Consider the book of Romans. What do we have here? On the one hand, it is simply a letter from Paul to the church in Rome. But just who was Paul? And who was the church of Rome? And just how does Paul's letter to the Romans express his relationship with this church? What is going on here? We ask these questions because it is *this letter* from *this apostle* to *this church* at *this point in time* that our almighty, heavenly Beloved has chosen as a vehicle of revelation.

Paul was a Jew, "circumcised on the eighth day ... as to righteousness under the law, blameless" (Phil 3:5-6). Yet he encountered the risen Christ, and the impact of this encounter changed him forever. Paul discovered that his acceptance by God was not dependent on his blameless Jewish behavior. Consequently, he found himself proclaiming this divine welcome not only to Jews but also to non-Jews, establishing communities of mutual support wherever a group received his message. The church at Rome, however, was not founded by Paul. Indeed, he had never visited Rome, though he hoped to visit soon. There was some tension between the Jewish and non-Jewish members of that community.

So, what is going on here? Some have looked at the book of Romans as Paul's "systematic theology," but certainly there is more there, given the circumstances. There is his desire to heal divisions within the church. There is his desire to clarify his own message so that he would not be misunderstood by others' reports of his views. There is his desire to advance the gospel further among the Romans and beyond. All of this and more is present in the letter to the Romans. The depths and nuances of Paul's own human relationship with God—and his hopes for Rome and the Christian church at large—are reflected in it. And just as the meaning of any human record is grasped with reference to the particulars of the object and the circumstances of its origin, those who wish to understand Romans are obliged to examine this human record with reference to the actual words of the text and the human historical context of its writing.

We can deepen our empathy for and connection with the characters of the Bible through studying biblical history. The effect of this study makes the story more interesting, more personal—all the facts, dates and archaeological details result in helping the *old* story become *our* story.

During Old Testament times, Lachish served as an important defensive outpost for Jerusalem. It blocked the most direct access route up from the coast. During the reign of Hezekiah, the Assyrians, led by King Sennacherib, laid siege to Jerusalem and captured Lachish (701 B.C.) (see 2 Chron 32:9; Is 36:2). Archaeology has shown that this was a brutal battle. The Assyrians built a stone and dirt ramp up to the level of the city wall and attacked the gates with battering rams and fire. There is a thick burn layer over the entire city, and excavations revealed 1,500 skulls in one of the caves near the site and hundreds of arrowheads on the ramp and at the top of the city wall.

As I stood on the ruins of this site and saw the evidence of this destruction and as I witnessed the human drama captured in the writing on some pottery fragments, I came to realize that these were people like me. They had families and hopes and dreams. They were not just inhabitants of some far away Bible Times Land. After learning of the destruction of this city and after pondering it with tears, I came to understand that these are *my* people. These people of faith are not just ancients, but people of a shared faith and a shared humanity, who knew the terror of waiting for an attack by an overwhelming enemy who ultimately overran their city—a city that was never again to be permanently rebuilt.

Some of Paul's writings are not easy to understand. Certain statements can be problematic. Nevertheless, it would be silly to give up hope of ever making any sense of Paul. This is true of any brilliant writer. Instead of giving up in despair, we read carefully, trying to catch something of the spirit of Paul's relationship with God expressed in this letter. We ponder the text, word by word. Perhaps we make an outline of the text. Perhaps we look to others who have studied this book more carefully. We leave the most difficult material for later. And we listen with our spirit, because this record—just one letter out of all that Paul may have written—is one of God's chosen means to invite us into love.

INVITATION TO RELATIONSHIP WITH GOD

But still there is more. Paul sent the letter to the Romans, hoping it would *do* something—perhaps many things. Relationship with God is not only expressed in the *creation* of Scripture, it is also part of the *intention* of

Scripture. Consider that to understand Romans as Paul would have wanted his letter understood is to grasp the kinds of ordinary human changes—in thought, feeling, action—encouraged in it. Also consider that the book of Revelation is designed to enthrall us in the imagination of heaven and to adjust our lives accordingly. The denunciations of the prophets are structured to grip us with a sense of condemnation and sincere repentance.

Albrecht Bengel (1687-1752), one of the pioneers of the scientific study of the Bible, spoke of the wonderful mix of doctrine, feeling and character in the text. He stated that "it is generally such that one can more easily reach it [a comprehension of the Scripture] by a perception of the heart than by a circuit of words." Thus Scripture is not merely—from the point of view of the human authors—an artifact of spirituality, an antique record of relationship with God. It also—as a human document—communicates desires, hopes and more. It is an invitation to spirituality, goading the readers to think, feel and act ever more deeply in relationship with God.

The sacred Christian Scriptures are written records of human beings' encounters with the living God. At the same time, these very texts have been assembled by God as a way of communicating his love. They are also invitations to relationship, written so that the readers might grow in spiritual life with God. Our longings.

Holy Scripture. New life. This is the formula. We long for living water, for truth, for transformation. We immerse ourselves in the text of Scripture: reading, meditating, praying, contemplating and acting. As a result of this practice, we receive life from God for ourselves and for others. Our wants are remade and fulfilled. Our minds are enlightened such that we are wiser than our elders. Our lives begin more and more to exhibit the values of our Creator.

By attending with care to the particulars of the text and by opening ourselves to the S/spirit of the text, we begin to sink our roots deep into the streams of water. To do so, however, requires some attention to our roots, and to *us*. In the next chapter, we will reflect on we who are reading.

3

WE WHO LIVE AND READ

One of the most common subjects of devotion throughout Christian history is the death of Christ. The events of that day receive more treatment—in four Gospels—than any other day in Scripture. Men and women have knelt before crosses or sat with Gospels in hand, and rehearsed that story again and again. We bring ourselves to the cross, and the Spirit of the risen Savior comes to minister to us in our meditation.

A number of years ago, a woman was participating in a spiritual retreat. As part of that retreat, she was to spend some time meditating on the death of Jesus: reading the passages and imaginatively being present with the events. Here's how she described her experience:

> We were asked to be a person at Jesus' death, you know ... to participate in that death. And how we felt as a person that participated there. Who were you and how did you feel, how did you react? Well, what really got to me, is that the pain and suffering that Jesus felt on that cross, ... it was like all the pain and suffering in my life just hit me. And I didn't know what to do....

I sat right there near the altar and tears started coming and I'm saying, "This feeling, I don't like this feeling." ... I felt all this pain and suffering that Jesus did is like the pain and suffering in my life, ... but understand that Jesus died on that cross for all of us, for all the pain from all of us, ... for all the sufferings that we might ever imagine.... I don't think I could do that, you know.... But, you see, that touched me at that time and I think since then He's been touching me through all the suffering because it no longer makes me ask the question, "Why am I suffering so hard?" I just ask Jesus to come in there and be present with me because you already suffered for this.

Perhaps the best way to think of it is to see lectio divina as an encounter of three elements: the inspired text of Scripture, the Christian reader and the Holy Spirit. In the previous chapter, we saw that Scripture is thoroughly human (and must be read as the expression of the human authors) and yet is at the same time the word of God. Now we will explore the Christian who interacts with the text.

To begin lectio divina, it is helpful to understand something about the character of human experience and about a few skills we use in devotional reading. But even in discussing the human dimension, we cannot avoid speaking about God—for the Holy Spirit, who inspired the text of Scripture, also indwells the Christian reader. And the presence of the living Holy Spirit makes all the difference.

WE ARE NOT ALONE

The first thing you must know about the human dimension of lectio divina is that we who read the text are not alone in our reading. There is Someone whispering nearby as we read God's love letter. Our reading of Scripture is never simply a matter of interpreting a book. Rather it is an encounter between ourselves and with the Spirit of Christ through the act of engaging with a book. Consequently, to learn about ourselves as readers, we must first learn a little about the Holy Spirit.

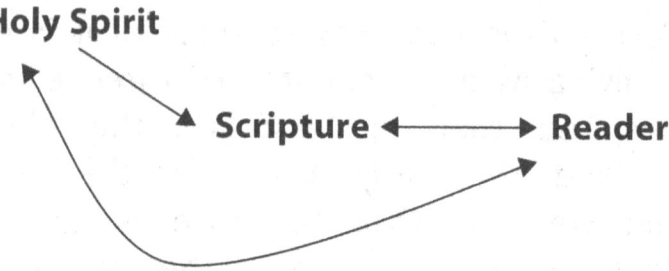

The Holy Spirit is God, the third person of the Trinity. As a *person*, the Spirit is described as having mind (Rom 8:27) and emotions (Eph 4:30). The Spirit of God is also described as a *force* or a wind (the terms for "spirit" in Hebrew and Greek can also be translated *wind* or *breath*). One way that Scripture describes entry into Christianity is to speak of "receiving the Spirit" or being "born" of the Spirit, identifying our connection with the influence of the Spirit of God as a defining feature of Christian life. The Spirit of God is, as a divine personal force, actively involved in human life. The Holy Spirit is particularly associated with communicating to us the heart and mind of God.

In the Nicene Creed, we recite that we believe in the Holy Spirit, "who has spoken through the prophets." Similarly, in Acts 13:1-2 we learn that in the midst of a gathering of prophets and church leaders "the Holy Spirit said" to set apart Barnabas and Saul for a mission. And again in John 16:14, Jesus states that when the Spirit of truth comes, he will "take what is mine and declare it to you." The Spirit spoke through the prophets and continues to speak directly with Christians today through the Scriptures and in various ways.

One way the Spirit communicates is by stimulating thoughts and feelings. Consider the following:
- The love of God is poured into our hearts through the Holy Spirit (Rom 5:5).
- The Spirit intercedes through us with unutterable sighs (Rom 8:26).
- The cry in our hearts reflects and expresses the Spirit (Rom 8:15; Gal 4:6).
- The Spirit interprets truth to our minds (1 Cor 2:11-13) and speaks particular instructions to some people (Acts 8:29).

- The Spirit of the Lord speaks through our dreams and visions (Acts 10:19) and through the gifted body of Christ (1 Cor 12:7-11).
- The Spirit acts as a powerful influence toward God, filling, leading, baptizing and sanctifying God's people.

In each of these examples, the Holy Spirit acts by addressing our thoughts and feelings. What this means is that we learn to recognize and to relate to the Spirit of God in lectio divina through attending to the thoughts and feelings that arise as we read. We bring *our* thoughts and feelings to our reading, and the Spirit causes *God's* thoughts and feelings to arise as we read.

WHAT WE BRING

What do we bring with us when we open our Bibles? Some of us may bring a pen or piece of paper. Some of us may bring a highlighter. But all of us bring our eyes, our questions, our situations, our thoughts and our feelings. It is easy to pay attention to our pen or highlighter when we read. It is not, however, as easy to pay attention to the eyes, questions, situations—the thoughts and feelings—we bring with us to our reading.

When we open the Bible, we read it in light of the way we look at things. Author Robert McAfee Brown says that we read Scripture with our own "eyes." For example, he notes that

Christians living in less developed regions notice different things in Scripture than Christians from more developed regions do. A Christian from a richer country might read the parable of the good Samaritan and notice the value of a random act of kindness shown to someone in need (seeing "neighbor" as the one helped). A Christian from a poorer country might read the same story and notice Jesus' affirmation of a style of life that intentionally acts compassionately toward the needy (seeing "neighbor" as the one helping). We come to Scripture with a heart and mind shaped by our global culture and local history. There are rich-neighborhood and poor-neighborhood eyes. There are medieval and modern eyes. There are male eyes and female eyes. Our political perspectives and our personal fears, our public education and our private meditation, our ordinary confusions and our deepest hopes—all accompany us as we open the Bible.

We also bring our questions to the text. Some of our questions are obvious. Perhaps we have even opened our Bible to explore a particular question ("What should we do when someone stands up in a church service and prays out loud in tongues?"). Other questions we bring are less obvious, or less conscious. For example, I am not sure how the Old Testament relates to the New. I believe God "never leaves us or forsakes us," but sometimes I feel forsaken. Some questions are a mere niggling in our side.

Others—perhaps hidden even deeper—threaten the foundations of our faith. Nevertheless, whether we are aware of them or not, our questions accompany us as we open the Bible.

Finally, we also bring our circumstances to our reading. Sometimes our circumstances are front and center. We are in desperate straits and come to the Scriptures in the midst of our plight. In such times it is natural to read the Scriptures *in terms of* our circumstances. One young man, for example, came to visit my property for a time of retreat and reflection. His wife had recently left him, moving to a distant city to explore life on her own. He was devastated by this and did not know what to do. Questions of divorce papers, future location, career and more were swirling about in his mind.

He communicated his predicament to others, and someone referred him to me. I told him that I was not a marriage counselor, but that I could provide space—and a listening ear—if he wanted to work on his relationship with God in the midst of this crisis. He said that this was actually just what he wanted, and so he came for a visit. One of his practices during this time was to read Scripture (he chose the book of John), and one day he found himself reading the story of the raising of Lazarus (Jn 11).

He said of this time of meditation, "I could not help but place my own situation onto the situation in the Scriptures." Here was Jesus, *waiting* when someone else had just died.

Lazarus's crisis was worse than his. He was dead. And here Jesus intentionally let things go a bit further. "I knew what it felt like to have the chips stacked against you," my friend said, "but this was a seriously hopeless situation." And Jesus did nothing. He let things take their own course. He let that death really sink in. And yet when he arrived on the scene, Jesus was not unfeeling toward the situation. He wept. Even though he may have seen how God's greater glory would be served by his own waiting, he still cared and expressed that care deeply. "Ultimately," my friend confessed, "I saw how Jesus was able to restore life to dead situations. In fact, perhaps it is better, at times, to let things really die so that God can raise it to new life."

Perhaps there are times when we need to be willing to sacrifice our own understanding of how God should work, knowing it is better to be willing to let something die so that God can raise it to new life *if that's how he chooses to go about doing it.* My young friend did what any godly man would do in such a time: he turned to Scripture and saw in the text anything that might speak to him of his situation. Indeed, as his reflection on this passage developed further, he wondered if he might not be making the whole interpretation up just to support a potential course of action. But then he realized that he had read lots of passages during the week, and that this one hit him with a different sense of conviction. His understanding was fair to the text, and it was a blow directly to his heart. Perhaps it was time to wait and see what God might do.

At other times, our circumstances are present but only in the back of our minds as we read a passage. Yet the Bible speaks to a circumstance. I remember one season when I was considering a change in my situation. I had gone to seminary with the intention of joining an urban pastoral training program. Honestly, I had my eyes set on being the next urban Christian hero, valiantly moving into the slums and saving the world.

One morning in my devotions, I turned to the passage for the day and found myself in 1 Kings 19, the story of Elijah hiding and God appearing before him. I wasn't consciously opening this passage to explore my situation, nor was my situation at the forefront of my mind that day. I just opened my Bible to the passage that was on my schedule. So I started reading, and I heard about God confronting Elijah. God asked, "What are you doing here, Elijah?" And Elijah responded, "I have been very zealous for the Lord ... I am alone am left" (1 Kings 19:9-10). Now I was awake. I could really identify with Elijah: zealous for the Lord, yet feeling alone in my commitments. So few people were willing, like *I was*, to make this radical commitment to Jesus. I finished the passage, but my mind wandered off and one thing led to another.

But later during that prayer time I became convicted by God *not* to pursue the urban training program. At the end of this experience of conviction, my thoughts were led back (God drew me back) to the passage I had read earlier, but had not really noticed. At the end of his confrontation with Elijah, God informed him, "Yet I will leave seven thousand in Israel, all the knees that have not bowed to Baal" (1 Kings 19:18). Was Elijah really "alone" out there serving God? No. In fact, he had an oversized estimation of his place in the world. And God, with this casual report, put Elijah in his place.

Frankly, I was put in my place as I reread this passage. Just who did I think I was? Would the inner cities of the world collapse if I did not attend this program? I had not opened my Bible that morning with my situation consciously in view, but it was there, and God used what I brought—however much in the background—to bring his own guidance to my life.

In summary, we come to Scripture reading with all of who we are, all of our thoughts and feelings. Our relationships, our activities, our hopes and much more are all present with us as we come to Scripture. We bring them with us to the text.

WHAT THE SPIRIT BRINGS

Remember that lectio divina is an encounter of Spirit, text and reader. You can think of the

Spirit as "coming to the meeting" when you open your Bible. And, in attending our meeting, the Spirit brings some things.

Sometimes it seems perfectly ordinary. You turn to a passage and read it. You think about this or that phrase. Perhaps you check a dictionary or a commentary for insight. Perhaps as you ponder the text an idea enters your mind that helps explain what you were wondering about. For example, you never really knew who the Samaritans were, and so you look it up. Now that you know that they were hated by the Jews, it helps you understand what Jesus was saying in the parable of the good Samaritan. Along with this new way of looking at Samaritans—and at the passage—there is born the beginnings of a new way of acting toward those you might naturally dislike.

What (or *who*) gave birth to this inclination? Be alert. What may seem perfectly natural is really supernatural. Why were you led to investigate the Samaritans? Just how was that new way of looking or acting born? It is not that you thought everything all out right there, while you were reading. The truth is that in the reading and the understanding, a new little inclination of openness toward others sparked to life.

Or perhaps you turn to the first epistle of Peter and read his warning not to "repay evil for evil or abuse for abuse; but on the contrary, repay with a blessing" (1 Pet 3:9). As you read the passage, you might be aware that you have not made repayment-with-blessing a practice, and you decide to change and try to make a habit of returning blessing for those who seek to do you ill. You simply apply the commandment of the passage to your life and go on with your reading. Now reflect again: just where did that awareness that you have not made Peter's command a practice in your life come from? The Spirit of God communicates by stimulating thoughts and feelings. Our simple acts of biblical and moral reasoning are often the means through which the Spirit of God speaks. The ordinary may actually be more extra-ordinary than we can imagine.

Then there are those moments when a hearing of the word of God changes our lives in a moment. Antony of Egypt (295-373) had been pondering the freedom of the early followers of Jesus when he went into church and heard the Gospel read. He heard the Lord saying to the rich man, "If you would be perfect, go, sell what you possess and give to the poor, and you will have treasure in heaven" (Mt 19:21). Athanasius, Antony's biographer, writes of Antony's response: "It was as if ... the passage were read on his account. Immediately Antony went out from the Lord's house and gave to the townspeople the possessions he had."

In a similar manner, John Wesley (1703-1791), evangelist and founder of the Methodists, felt his heart "strangely warmed" as he heard a passage of Luther's preface to Paul's epistle to the Romans read in a small gathering. The passage spoke of the change God works in the heart through faith in Christ. Wesley felt an assurance that Christ had taken away *his* sins personally and saved him from the law of sin and death. He was never the same after that encounter with Scripture. Sometimes when we come to Scripture, the Spirit brings a complete makeover.

Quite often, however, the Spirit's offerings fall between these two extremes: not just ordinary Bible application but not a life-changing moment either. Such was the case with Ignatius of Loyola (1491-1556). Ignatius was a soldier who had been injured during a battle and was forced to lie in bed for an extended period of recovery. He had only two books to read during his time of recuperation: a life of Christ and a history of the saints of the church (not necessarily his favorite reading). As he rested, he would think periodically about his readings. At other times he would fantasize about a young woman in whom he was interested and about other worldly adventures.

After a while, Ignatius noticed something about his own musings. To paraphrase his own words, "When he was thinking of those things of the world he took much delight in them, but afterward ... he found himself dry and dissatisfied. But when he thought of imitating the sacrifices of Christ and the saints of the church not only was he consoled when he had those thoughts, but even after putting them aside he remained satisfied and joyful." This season of reading and reflecting was Ignatius's first lesson in recognizing the movements of the Spirit of God.

Over time Ignatius of Loyola penned a manual of biblical meditation called *The Spiritual Exercises*. The *Exercises* are rooted in a practice of reading (and rereading) Scripture, along with paying close attention to the thoughts and feelings that arise in the context of that reading. Ignatius—and many others who have followed him—have learned that the Holy Spirit introduces thoughts, feelings and inclinations into our experience in harmony with our own growth and situation.

For example, I might read of Abraham's obedience and become attracted myself to the life of abandoned obedience. This interest grows as I read elsewhere, but I am uncertain where that obedience is to find its concrete expression. Months later, I find out that my mother is seriously ill, and I will need to make serious adjustments to care for her. Thanks to my Holy Spirit preparation through lectio divina, I am ready to give myself to this life of abandoned obedience (just as Abraham did) and care for my mother, no matter what the costs.

I read another passage of Scripture and may sense a slight feeling of fear or threat when I hear Jesus asking us to consider the lilies of the field. Again, it may take time to discover what this fear is about, as the Spirit invites me to recognize my lack of trust in a matter. The deeper things of our souls do not readily come to the surface, and the Spirit's voice can be subtle. But with patience and careful attention, we can learn to notice both the movements of our own souls and the Spirit's work as we engage with Scripture.

WHAT THE SPIRIT DOES

We come with *our* thoughts and feelings to our reading, and the Spirit causes *God's* thoughts and feelings to arise as we read. In time, the Spirit reorders the thoughts and feelings of our heart.

We all use "heart" language. "Her comment cut me to the heart." "Now we will discuss the heart of the matter." "She has a heart of stone." We often see the heart as the seat of emotion and imagine it at odds with the head. Yet in our examples above (and for many biblical writers and ancient Christians) the heart is the seat of the mind, will and emotions. The heart is the control center of the whole life. The language of the heart, however, is more evocative than precise.

Perhaps the closest equivalent for capturing this sense is to say that the heart contains our motives; it is the engine that drives us. The heart motivates us. It is the equivalent to character, core personality or motivational structures. In the heart reside the answers to the questions "What have you set your hopes on?" "What gives you meaning?" At times the answers etched in our hearts differ from those we speak with our lips; nevertheless, the heart holds the steering wheel.

The heart—this center of personality and motivation—is what we bring to our devotional reading of Scripture. Whether we are Pharisees motivated by our desire to remain on top of our own religious circle or we are widows burdened by loneliness and the struggle to survive, our very reading and interpretation of Scripture is shaped by the hearts we bring to the text, and as we are open to the text, we expose our hearts to the Holy Spirit, the agent of change and healing.

Perhaps we could think of the heart as an old "operating system" of our life. It's not just that the data of life accumulates and we need a bit more memory, or that the machine gets hot and we need a little rest. We must realize that as human beings—halfway between earth and heaven—our whole way of seeing and interpreting the data of life is faulty. Our basic system of putting things together, making sense of things, is inadequate and in need of replacement. The good news we find in the Bible and in the Christian tradition is that our hearts can be changed. The Lord God promises through the prophet Ezekiel that "a new heart I will give you, and a new spirit I will put within you; and I will remove from your body the heart of stone and give you a heart of flesh" (Ezek 36:26).

There are aspects of this reordering that seem to just happen. One man invites God to come and rule his life and finds himself experiencing a new birth. He wakes up the next morning to find a new meaning in life. At other times, we must invest in this change. A young woman chooses to live wisely and discovers over time, as Proverbs suggests, that the good life is self-reinforcing: her heart becomes what she practices.

Yes, as with all operating systems, there are revisions, updates and such that are needed along the way. Our hearts, like our computers' operating systems, require periodic reprogramming and regular maintenance. The Lord God who promises to give us a new heart will also strengthen it. As Paul prayed for the Thessalonians, "And may he so strengthen your hearts in holiness that you may be blameless before our God and Father at the coming of our Lord Jesus with all his saints" (1 Thess 3:13).

There are a number of activities through which we cooperate with the Spirit's heart-reprogramming. We rehearse our worldview through liturgy and worship. We meditate on truth, and it begins to soak in. We take our hands off the steering wheel of life and trust God to care for things. We live intentionally, at odds with the dominant culture and that intention—in tension—reinforces a new life. We suffer well, perhaps even enduring persecution, and this reinforces our values as well. Encounters with God, authentic repentance, music, attentiveness to our own thoughts—we could go on and on. The point we wish to make here is that in the practice of lectio divina, we actually do a number of these activities. Divine reading is a powerful tool for reprogramming our hearts.

Let's ponder this. Lectio divina originates from a tradition of liturgical reading and worship. We may use the New Testament reading from our communal Morning Prayer as the focus of a time of solitude. Or if we are in a time of private worship, our liturgy and our lectio become the same act. We sit with the passage and meditate. We repent when we find ourselves falling short of what we read. We may chant the passage or sing a Scripture song that goes with the text, and the music brings the word still deeper. We stop as we read and attend to our thoughts. "Why do I often struggle with this passage?"

Rather than living on in mindless autopilot, where our pace of life or our addictions to media and distractions pull us from the reality of the moment, we choose, in lectio, to focus on our being present to the present—being present with this text right here, in my life right here. An exercise like this can help us become grateful for the life we have been given, and this gratefulness can, in turn, open our hearts to appreciate and love God more deeply.

Lectio can also fuel our vision of Christ and Christlike living. We read a section of the Gospels and slowly get in touch with the drama of the passage: A widow's grief. Jesus stops. He cares and heals. We have felt Jesus' compassion, and we want to care like that as well. Through this act of reading, our heart is strengthened in holiness. This is the Spirit, the text and the reader encountering each other together.

The elders of the desert recognized this connection of the heart to Scripture. Abba Moses, for example, in a conversation with John Cassian in the fourth century, summarized the life of the desert by saying,

> Everything we do, our every objective, must be undertaken for the sake of this purity of heart.... For this we must practice the reading of Scripture, together with all the other virtuous activities, and we do so to trap and to hold our hearts free of harm of every dangerous passion and in order to rise step by step to the high point of love.

The desert elders encouraged a practice of watchfulness, paying attention to what thoughts arise as we sit and read, and as we live life generally. We learn to "guard [our] heart" (Prov 4:23 TNIV) by watching and redirecting our thoughts to subjects that are true, honorable, just, pure, pleasing, commendable and worthy of praise (Phil 4:8) rather than on those thoughts that bring anxiety, defensiveness, judgment or self-protection. The very act of choosing to read

Scripture is an act of redirecting our thoughts to the things of God. But we also find ourselves watching and redirecting our thoughts while we are in the midst of the act of reading Scripture. In doing so, we attend to the work of the Spirit of God, who communicates by stimulating thoughts and feelings in our experience.

For example, you may want to ask yourself a few questions while (or after) you read a passage of Scripture as a way to help you be aware of the Spirit's work:

- What have I been thinking about as I have read this passage? Why?
- Are there any particular thoughts, questions or ideas that have come up?
- Have I noticed any graces or sins in my life as I have been reading? What kinds of responses do I notice?
- What have I seen of the Lord in my reading, of God's character or works? How am I led to respond to what I see of God?
- Do I notice any inclinations to action as I read this passage? What might be underneath these inclinations?
- What feelings have accompanied my reading? Why?

These questions give us a sample of a lectio-cultivated watchfulness. This kind of watchfulness, in turn, facilitates that place in life where we are able to insert a moment of reflection between a thought arising and our acting on it. Here we are less reactive, less volatile, less prejudiced and more able to act out of our love rather than out of hurt or anger. Watchfulness provides a path to freedom from destructive thoughts and emotions. It cultivates our ability to allow our minds to dwell on those things that are helpful and good. In time, our hearts themselves are reformed.

Lectio divina, or devotional reading, engages the human dimension with the Word and the Spirit of God. We bring ourselves to the text: eyes, questions, circumstances, heart—all of us. We watch as we read, noticing how the reading process is shaped by the Spirit. We allow the Scripture to soak into us and reprogram our heart, changing the very concerns and ideas that control our beliefs and feelings. Through this process, our ordinary questions, our cultural biases, our personal fears and our controlling operating systems are placed at the disposal of God's Spirit through the text. And through the same process, our mind is renewed and our heart is transformed. In the chapters ahead, we will explore five separate elements of this practice: reading, meditating, praying, contemplating and acting.

4
READING

In the course of a day, we read many different things, and we read them in many different ways. We scan through a catalog, looking for one piece of information. We browse a newspaper, our eyes meandering around the pages. We pore over a technical essay, reading the same lines again and again to grasp their meaning. We proofread, we speed read, and sometimes we just curl up in a lazy chair for the pleasure of reading. Christians also read the Scriptures in different ways. We study it at home, and we hear it at church. We turn the pages of the Gospels like a gripping novel, or we sit with a psalm like a rich poem. One common way of reading Scripture—and the way we are highlighting here—is devotional reading (lectio divina).

Lectio divina is the reading of a lover: the relaxed waiting that is as attentive to the relationship as it is to the text. Though not divorced from analytical study, it is slower and more meditative. It is where reading and prayer are bound together. It is a reading that comes out of a life with God and leads into life with God. Eighteenth-century British Nonconformist author Philip Doddridge (1702-1751) encouraged just this kind of reading in his influential *The Rise and Progress of Religion in a Soul.* He advised:

> Read some portion of Scripture: not a great deal, nor the whole Bible in its course; but some select portions out of its most useful parts, perhaps ten or twelve verses, ... considering them merely in a devotional and practical view. Here take such instructions as readily present themselves to your thoughts, repeat them over to your own conscience, and charge your heart religiously to observe them, and act upon them.... And if you pray over the substance of this Scripture with your Bible open before you, it may impress your memory and your heart yet more deeply, and may form you to a variety, both of thought and expression, in prayer.

Notice the process Doddridge describes and the terms he uses. Read a small, select portion. Consider this portion in a devotional and practical view, an eye to your relationship and response to the God who is revealed through the text. Be ready for some "instructions" to present themselves to your thoughts as you read. When they do appear, spend time with them, respond to them. As you do this, these impressions will work their way deeper and deeper into your life and will change the way you pray. This is lectio divina.

In earlier chapters, we described lectio divina as an approach that contains a number of elements or "ways of being with" the text: reading, meditating, praying, waiting and resting and acting in the midst of the trials of life. These elements are not strictly distinct tasks or stages, but rather are general components of an integrated process of being with God through Scripture. Just as all our methods of interacting with Scripture (study, hearing, meditation and so on) contribute to a full hearing of the word of God through the text, so the various elements of this particular method of divine reading work together to create an atmosphere of devotion within which our relationship with God can be uniquely fostered. In this chapter we will explore the element of *reading*.

WHAT IS READING LIKE?

We use the phrase "lectio divina" generally to describe the practice of ordinary devotional interaction with Scripture. We also identify *reading* as a single act within this larger practice, namely, the act of exposing ourselves to the text. What is reading (exposing ourselves to the text) like, especially as one component of a larger process of lectio divina?

I pick up my Bible and turn to a passage. Perhaps I have been reading through the Gospel of Luke, and today's passage is Luke 5:17-26. Just for fun, I decide to read it out loud. "One day, while he was teaching, Pharisees and teachers of the law were sitting near by...; and the power of the Lord was with him to heal." I stop. I think a little. *What does it mean, "the power of the Lord was with him to heal"? Was this some special moment? Wasn't the power of God always with Jesus?* After trying out a few different ideas, I decide that I can't solve this.

So I read on, slowly, phrase by phrase. "Just then some men came, carrying a paralyzed man on a bed. They were trying to bring him in and lay him before Jesus; but finding no way to bring him in because of the crowd, they went up on the roof and let him down with his bed through the tiles into the middle of the crowd in front of Jesus." As I read this section, I picture the scene: the building, the men carrying the bed with the paralytic, the crowd. I identify with the frustration of those men carrying the bed and their inability to get through the crowd. I see them climbing on the roof. But then I wonder, *What were roofs like in those days? What did these "tiles" look like, and how did the men remove them to let their friend down? Did it make a lot of noise?* (And so on.)

Once again, I imagine a few options, based on my experience of roofs. I decide to look up this detail in a Bible dictionary someday—but not just now. I wonder who these men were who carried the paralytic. *Were they family or friends?* I remember that I need to write my sister on Facebook and wish her a happy birthday. But now I am reading. *I am here with you, God.*

So where was I? Oh, yeah, they set him in front of Jesus. "When he saw their faith he said, 'Friend, your sins are forgiven you.' Then the scribes and the Pharisees began to question." *I imagine the Pharisees murmuring among themselves,* "Who can forgive sins but God alone?" *Other passages about forgiveness come to mind. And then I remember last year. What I did last year was stupid. I know it was wrong. Some people at work still haven't forgiven me. My mind travels back in memory. And then back to the passage, to Jesus telling that paralyzed man that his sins were forgiven.* "He said to the one paralyzed—'I say to you, stand up and take your bed and go to your home.'"

I think, I've been paralyzed ever since that event. I just can't seem to move forward, or even stand up. I wish I could stand up. I'm here, God. How does this forgiveness and healing thing work? Then I hear that phrase of Jesus again: "Friend, your sins are forgiven you." *But this time I hear him speaking not to the paralytic in the story, but to me. It is as if Jesus is looking down on me, lying on my own bed of sin, unable to move. I feel him calling me* "friend." *For a few moments, my distractions are gone, and there I am facing Jesus who looks at me and tells me my sins are forgiven.*

I return to the passage. "Immediately he stood up before them, took what he had been lying on, and went to his home, glorifying God. Amazement seized all of them, and they glorified

God and were filled with awe, saying, 'We have seen strange things today.'" This passage reminds me of the one I read the other day in Luke 2, where the angels and the shepherds glorified God for sending Jesus. Again, I think, *Something happened to that man, something that connected his forgiveness and his healing, his ability to stand up and go. Jesus talked about "authority" in the passage. What the Pharisees were concerned about did not matter. What mattered was what Jesus said. And Jesus tells me my sins are forgiven. I think I'll try to stand up.*

I close the book and go on with my day. And when, at work, I am confronted with that same old feeling of shame, I stand up a little bit. I refuse to let my past failures define me and my relationships with others. *Jesus has forgiven me, and in his forgiveness I can get on with life.*

READING AND INTERPRETING

As we mentioned above, we are considering reading as the basic act of exposing ourselves to the text. Something like the process above goes on when we expose ourselves to the text of Scripture. We can see hints of the other elements in the story. *Prayer* is present, along with a sense of the *contemplative* perception of the Lord's forgiveness. *Action* is behind the scene as "the event" of the past and the direction of change for the future. There is actually little *meditation*, as we will learn in the following chapter. Nevertheless, our aim in telling this story is simply to give you a sense of what ordinary devotional reading (exposure to the text) is like.

But there may be some problems with my reading of the story above, problems that illustrate the tensions between informational and devotional readings of the Scripture, problems that help us learn more about the relationship between sacred text and life. Let's take a closer look.

If we look carefully at the book of Luke, we find that 4:31–6:11 is a collection of stories about Jesus' authority and character. In 4:14-30, Jesus has returned from the temptation in the wilderness "filled with the power of the Spirit." He proclaims in his own hometown his own fulfillment of the prophecy of Isaiah—that he is the anointed one who would proclaim good news to the poor, release captives, heal the sick and usher in a new era for God's people. Jesus' own townspeople do not believe him and try to throw him off a cliff, but he slips away and begins an itinerant ministry.

Then we have the stories: Jesus teaches and people are astounded. Jesus casts out demons, and the demons proclaim him to be the Holy One of God. Jesus heals. Jesus causes fish to multiply and multitudes follow him. Jesus welcomes the worst of society and offers good news to the least. We notice the characters in the plot: the crowd that is "astounded," the

Pharisees and hometown crowd who reject Jesus, the people who choose to follow him.

Remember our discussion of the *word of God* through *human words* in chapter two? Luke structured these stories (human words) to demonstrate the divine authority of Jesus and the different possible responses to this God-man. The point of the story of the paralytic for Luke is not simply the man's forgiveness, but the breadth of Jesus' divine authority. Yes, he heals, he casts out demons, he causes fish to appear, but these can be performed by wonderworkers or prophets. Forgiving sins, however, can be accomplished "by God alone." It is this, combined with Jesus' healing and the crowd's amazement ("we have seen strange things"), that brings Luke's point home.

A careful study of repeated words, character structure and literary plot development show us that this passage was written to contribute to a larger statement about Jesus' divine character and our response. It was written to give us one more piece of evidence regarding Jesus (see Lk 1:1-4). We could say that this proclamation of Jesus' character is what Luke intended the passage to *mean*.

But was my focus on Jesus' forgiveness out of place? Was my personal identification with the paralytic misguided? Am I wrong to get what I did out of this passage in my time of devotional reading? Does the more imaginative, intuitive, devotional reading of Scripture tend to lead us astray from the clear meaning of the text established through grammatical and historical study? On all these questions we would answer, "Not necessarily." We would say that a devotional reading of Scripture enables the discovery of both the primary intended meanings of the text and any number of accompanying implications in ways that other, more rational approaches cannot uncover. Let's look further.

It is only natural for the human mind to follow verbal and conceptual triggers. One "hook word" associates with another—as author Jean Leclercq described words in monastic reading that link passages or ideas—and the understanding of a passage builds not through logical analysis but rather through a notentirely-random accumulation of passages, ideas and experiences surrounding the passage at hand. Psychologists who study the human brain and nervous system speak about the development and spread of neural networks. Our mind naturally tends to follow associations that are strongly connected.

But just because it is natural, does that make it *right*? Perhaps yes, perhaps no. Let's look further. True, Luke's point in this passage was to build evidence for Jesus' divinity and for the value of following him. As we see in the stories that precede and follow this one, Luke piled up story after story to show Jesus' divine anointing. Jesus heals; Jesus casts out demons; Jesus works changes in the physical universe; even Jesus' teaching is different. And then on top of it all, here Jesus claims to *forgive sins,* something everyone knew (and the Pharisees most of all) could be provided only by God. Luke was clearly building a case for the divine messiahship of Jesus.

But along the way, Luke does tell us that *Jesus forgives sins.* It is not the primary point, but it is a legitimate affirmation along the way. And along the way, Luke also tells us that in some mysterious way our forgiveness and our healing are somehow connected in the Messiah. These are matters that any good scholar would affirm as contributing to the whole truth of Luke's message.

But in my devotional reading, I grasp this point in a different way. What is understood through a scholarly analysis of the text as a legitimate implication of Luke's writing is grasped through my devotional reading of the text more intuitively and with emphasis. Jesus forgives sins. Jesus forgives *my* sins. Jesus heals. Jesus can heal *me.* Needless to say, a deeper understanding of Jesus' forgiveness and healing facilitates our trust in those other features of his divine anointing. In the end, though my reading may seem to be about me and my sense of forgiveness by God (a relational reorientation), it also leads to a new sense of appreciation for Jesus which, of course, *is* Luke's primary point.

Whether we approach reading as academic exploration or as relational communication, we pay attention to things. We just pay attention to different phenomena in each case. Liturgical exposure to Scripture, singing Scripture, meditation of Scripture, study of Scripture—these all have their place and their functions. Each must be employed to serve and to contribute to the others.

PERSONAL INTERPRETATION AND THE HOLY SPIRIT

But isn't lectio divina a bit dangerous, just allowing anybody (or any group) to sit in front of a Bible, read a little passage and get out of it what comes up in their mind? Isn't this reading—the open exposure to Scripture—even somewhat presumptuous? Don't people need priests or scholars or precise exegetical techniques to interpret the Bible? What is to keep them from heresy?

These are precisely the questions asked by Pietist leader Philipp Spener (1635-1705) in his defense of lay participation in the service of Christ. His answer begins as follows:

> First of all the principal points of doctrine and rules of life are given in the Scriptures so clearly and according to the letter that each uneducated person can learn and comprehend them as well as the learned. Thus when pious hearts have comprehended these and obediently used the first measure received, as they continue to read the Scriptures with meditation and

prayer, God the Holy Spirit will open their understanding more and more, so that they may also learn and understand the higher and higher and more difficult matters as far as is necessary for strengthening of their faith, instruction in life, and comfort (Matt. 13:12; John 14:21; 2 Tim. 3:15-17).

Spener was careful to encourage pastoral participation in Bible study groups. And of course, it is one thing for a person to explore a text for personal edification in private devotion and another when we develop policies or statements of faith for larger communities. In the latter case, we must employ means of reading the text that are publicly shared and adjudicated. Still, we all have our own gift to offer to the church's comprehension of Scripture, and we have our own ways of receiving from the text. We leave ourselves and others all the poorer when we don't permit everyone to explore the Word of God.

DOING LECTIO ON TOUGH PASSAGES

What about the passages where Scripture appears to be contradictory or those difficult matters we discover in our reading? One suggestion for our reading at these points is to rest in what we do know, trusting God (perhaps through others) to illumine us concerning what we *don't* know. When we were in college, discussion of the "end times" was of particular interest. In the midst of this incessant discussion, I decided to figure things out for myself and to read through the book of Revelation. I remember almost despairing when I read chapter twelve about a dragon and a woman fleeing into the wilderness. I was almost bitter about how confusing the text was, and then someone I trusted admonished me to sit with what I could understand in the passage. The words from Revelation 12:10 almost leapt off the page:

Then I heard a loud voice in heaven, proclaiming,

"Now have come the salvation and the power
    and the kingdom of our God
    and the authority of his Messiah,
for the accuser of our comrades has been thrown down,
who accuses them day and night before our God."

Here were words I could understand, and these were the words I needed. I needed to hear that ringing declaration of victory through Jesus. I desperately needed to hear Satan described as my accuser and to realize that my guilt-induced scrupulosity was the result of his accusations and not Spirit-born conviction.

Evangelical Anglican Edward Bickersteth (1786-1850) gave helpful advice regarding this in his *A Scripture Help*.

We must not fancy, because one text, at first sight, appears to contradict another, that therefore it does so. Let us not so much as suppose that the Scripture can differ from itself, but humbly wait upon God till we can better reconcile one text with another. We shall find that in so doing, gospel truths will open themselves to our minds more and more, and we shall come by degrees to *the unity of faith and of the knowledge of the son of God*, spoken of, Eph. iv. 13.

In a similar vein, one of my professors said he learned to put these troubling passages safely away temporarily into a mental refrigerator. In this mental refrigerator, these passages did not spoil and sour his thinking, but they were available for him to revisit and explore as he developed a richer and more nuanced understanding that could help him understand them.

Another way of looking at our experience of difficulty in the text of Scripture is to receive our struggle as an inviting challenge from God. Thomas Merton suggested,

For most people, the understanding of the Bible is, and should be, a struggle: not merely to find meanings that can be looked up in books of reference, but to come to terms personally with the stark scandal and contradiction in the Bible itself. It should not be our aim merely to explain these contradictions away, but rather to use them as ways to enter into the strange and paradoxical world of meanings and experiences that are beyond us and yet often extremely and mysteriously relevant to us.

Too often we seem to have the idea that submission to Scripture means that we first come to see it as reasonable and then submit to it, but submission means, in part, a willingness to bend the knee in faith to things that are not fully resolved in our mind. Rich Mullins captured this perspective when he wrote about the creed: "I did not make it, no it is making me."

And this brings us to the notion of *illumination*. In chapter two we spoke of revelation and inspiration, two theological terms that help us understand something of what Scripture is. A third term, which describes more how we understand or even read Scripture, is *illumination*. The doctrine of the illumination of Scripture teaches that the Holy Spirit is active through our encounter with Scripture, revealing God within us (see, for example, Jn 14:26). Reading Scripture is never reading alone. There is always the voice of the Spirit nearby—both for individuals and for the community of God—whispering to us about the meaning of his love letter.

THE PRACTICE OF READING

Now that we have some sense of what reading involves and have affirmed its place in Christian devotion, it remains to give a few suggestions regarding the practice itself.

First, devotional reading, as any practice, is best accomplished with a little preparation. You might want to *start with the environment*. Do you know of a place and a time where you can focus on the text, leisurely, uninterrupted and free to respond to the movements of the Spirit? You might also want to consider your "mental environment" for reading Scripture. A good mental environment is when we are living out its truths in life. In this sense, sacred life leads to a clearer understanding of the sacred text. Concerning the relationships between our life, our approach to the Scriptures and our theology, Augustine remarked, "In the Scriptures, our eyes see with more or less clearness, according as we die more or less to this present world; and, on the contrary, in proportion as we live to this world, we do not discern spiritual things." Yet at the same time, we cannot make ourselves perfect before coming to God in Scripture. Indeed, that is part of the whole point: we come to Scripture in all our mixture of saved and sinner, waiting for the Word of God. So we do our best.

Next, as we prepare to read, it is good to *remember what we are bringing to the text.* Why are we picking up this book? What do we expect or hope to read? With what "eyes" do we come to the text? What mood do we bring to our reading today, and why? The state of our relationship with God is just as real in our reading and interpreting of Scripture as the state of our relationship with another person is present as we read and interpret his or her letters. Just as it is important in American football to have both a physical and a mental "set" before the ball is hiked, ready for what is to come, so it is helpful in lectio divina to prepare a little for the time of devotional reading. A resolve to *follow* Scripture will influence our very *reading* of Scripture.

It is also helpful to *have some means of writing nearby.* Sometimes we need only to record that reminder to write a birthday wish to our sister, and so remove that distraction from our mind. At other times we need to jot down a historical or a theological question to be explored elsewhere in commentaries or other resources. At times, more serious journal keeping can be a valuable vehicle for processing what is going on as we read a passage of Scripture (just so long as you don't get distracted).

It is also helpful, at times, to have some *easy-to-access resources* nearby. Study-Bible notes or a simple commentary can be searched quickly when an historical or grammatical question arises. We look it up and then get back to our devotions. Needless to say, we can be drawn into academic curiosity and lose our devotional reading altogether. Biblical language teacher Augustus Herman Franck warns against such ill-timed curiosity,

> lest a knowledge of *external* points render us less ardent and lively in reading the Word itself. How many are there who err in this respect, and feed contentedly on the husks, while those heavenly delights which flow from the Volume of Revelation remain untasted and unenjoyed....
>
> In the use of external helps, both deficiency and excess are blameable.... They are most secure who take the middle path; who neither rely on their own wisdom, nor are fascinated by the authority of others; but learn happily to conjoin Internal with External Helps.

And this leads us to our last suggestion: *read with humility*. On the one hand, God has seen fit to reveal himself to us through Scripture—to inspire the authors and to illumine the readers of the text. On the other hand, we are not infallible readers, and we must come to the text with a deep awareness of our weaknesses. We come to the text in humility when we are willing to hear the questions of another person and when we are open to hear the challenge of the divine Other.

A FINAL STORY

Again, the point of the matter is that in our exposure to the text, our heart joins with the work of God, who spoke and now illumines the Word to transform us today. Perhaps a story can help illustrate. In my college days, I was confused by my understanding of Scripture. I had earlier been taught that salvation was about a creed, a prayer and then a life of moral purity and active witnessing. But my college atmosphere emphasized issues like racial equality, peacemaking, world hunger and other social issues. In an effort to resolve my personal and theological confusion, I decided to expose myself to Scripture.

I took out my concordance and looked up every passage that had anything to do with these issues (wealth, oppression, poor, mammon, justice and so on). There were hundreds of passages, and this study took me over a year. I would read and meditate, read and meditate. I took a few notes as well. In the end, I never did answer the precise political questions I had hoped to answer. But when this study was over, I was a changed person.

Through exposing myself again and again to these passages, I got a sense for the heart of God: a God who reaches out in compassion, who hates injustice, who is generous and who longs for righteousness. I never gave up my creed or my sense of the importance of witnessing. Rather, thanks to my reading of the text (there was actually a combination of academic study and devotional reading present in this exploration), I can say that I experience a much richer identification with the God who created and cares about our social structures.

5
MEDITATING

The word *Meditation* may sound a bit exotic. You might even wonder, "Is it okay to meditate?" No worry, you are already doing it. While the Bible has a lot to say about meditation, it assumes that everyone meditates, just as it assumes that everyone worships. The Bible concerns itself with who or what we worship and with what we meditate about—directing our minds to Scripture, creation and redemption—but it *assumes* meditation rather than commands it. At the most basic level, meditation is our dwelling on, obsessing over, scheming about, daydreaming about or fantasizing over something we value. Think of the children's game in which you seek to move a ball through a maze, and one of the obstacles is a groove that diverts the ball away from the goal. The automatic meditations of our heart are like a well-worn groove that channels and directs the ball of our thinking.

This is why Jesus is so concerned about worry. Worry is a form of meditation. It is a way of practicing the presence of doubt and spiritual darkness as we actively question God's providential care for us. We do not have to say, "Let's set aside some time to worry and obsess over this." Worry just happens automatically. The worry groove diverts the ball of our thoughts, and we replay our fears again and again, even though we might say we agree with Jesus that worry is utterly futile for improving our lives (see Mt 6:24-35).

We all meditate—we all think about things that hook us. The psalmist called his automatic meditations "the meditation of my heart" (Ps 19:14), and he prayed that they, along with his words, would be pleasing to God. Whether they be unhealthy fears or godly tears, our thoughts return again and again to familiar thought paths. In fact, we often spend mental energy trying to turn off some of these seemingly automatic meditations.

Unlike the mind-chatter of automatic meditation, *intentional* meditation is deliberate and provides a way to change our automatic thoughts. The power of practiced meditation comes from the way it shapes our patterns of automatic thought, making them less negative and more appreciative of the grace that fills our lives, and changing their actual content, as our minds are filled with noble truths that restore and set us right. Christians have practiced many forms of intentional meditation through the ages; many of them are directly connected to the text of Scripture.

WHAT IS SCRIPTURE MEDITATION?

The most common biblical image for the Bible is "word." Specifically, the Bible is the Word of God, and this affirms that the Bible does its work through the medium of language. The Word has its unique authority and power because it is of God. Through his Word, God created the world, affected our redemption and shares his love. There is power in the words of Scripture, not because they are magically powerful in themselves; their power comes from the power of the speaker. This word has power because through it God acts—God blesses, judges, brings new life, protects, sets things right.

Through Scripture *reading,* we expose ourselves to the text. Through Scripture *meditation,* we allow the text to soak into us; we permit the influence or power of Scripture to act within. Isaiah proclaimed God's message: "My word ... shall not return empty" (Is 55:10-11). Jeremiah pictured God's word as a "fire" (Jer 5:14; 20:9) and a "hammer that breaks a rock in pieces" (Jer 23:29). The psalmist speaks of it as warning a person (Ps 19:11). "The word of the Lord came to..." is a common biblical phrase that denotes that the word has become a powerful guiding reality in someone. Scripture meditation, then, is a way to cultivate an openness to the word so that "the word of the

Lord comes" to you. This is perhaps akin to what the Virgin Mary did as she "pondered" in her heart the implications of Christ's incarnation (Lk 1:26-38).

When we think about the actual process of meditation, two ancient images have helped us. The first is *rumination*. Picture a cow, sheep or goat contentedly chewing its cud. These animals have a multipart stomach. Their food is partially digested in the first stomach and then regurgitated as cud, to be chewed once again to further break down the plant material. Ruminating was the image used by the monks who loved Scripture so much that they spent their lives copying it and praying it. They saw meditation as taking in Scripture by reading and memorizing it, and then bringing it back up to chew it again and again until it could be digested and fully used.

This chewing of the word, savoring it and leisurely dwelling with it, requires becoming very familiar with the word. Often this is done by focusing on an image, a phrase or even one word from the text at a time. Today we think of meditation as quiet and mental, but for many Christians, it was spoken and physical in the sense that attention was paid to posture and demeanor. Martin Luther urged that Christians "should meditate, that is not only in your heart, but also externally, by actually repeating and comparing oral speech and literal words of the book." Similarly, speaking of the early Christians of the desert, Douglas Burton-Christie wrote,

"Meditation was not, as the word has come to imply today, an interior reflection on the meaning of certain words. It was first and foremost the utterance, or exclamation of words, which were gradually digested and interiorized. Meditation on Scripture was an oral phenomenon. We see this in the account of witnesses, who are said to both *hear* and *see* monks meditating on Scripture."

The second image comes directly from Scripture. In the Old Testament, some of the chief words for meditation have a bodily dimension that is missing in our words like *brood, ponder* or *meditate*. The Old Testament words sometimes refer to the cooing of a dove or to the growl of a lion as it contentedly consumes its kill. Eugene Peterson captured this in his reflection on his dog's delight for gnawing bones.

> He gnawed the bone, turned it over and around, licked it, worried it. Sometimes we could hear a low rumble or growl, what in a cat would be a purr. He was obviously enjoying himself and in no hurry. After a leisurely couple of hours he would bury it and return the next day to take it up again. An average bone lasted about a week.
>
> I always took delight in my dog's delight, his playful seriousness, his childlike spontaneities now totally absorbed in "the one thing needful." ... [In Isaiah] I found the poet-prophet observing something similar to what I enjoyed so much in my dog, except

that his animal was a lion instead of a dog: "As a lion or young lion growls over his prey..." (Isa. 31:4). "Growls" is the word that caught my attention.... What my dog did over his precious bone, making those low throaty rumbles of pleasure as he gnawed, enjoyed, and savored his prize, Isaiah's lion did to his prey.... My delight was noticing the Hebrew word here translated as "growl" *(hagah)* but usually translated as "meditate," as in the Psalm 1 phrase describing the blessed man or woman whose "delight is in the law of the Lord," on which "he meditates day and night" (v. 2). Or in Psalm 63: "when I think of thee upon my bed, and meditate on thee in the watches of the night" (v. 6). But Isaiah uses this word to refer to a lion growling over his prey the way my dog worried a bone.

Rumination. Growling. Gnawing. What do these images mean for my practice of meditation? Rumination tells us that we need to know the text well enough that we can call it to mind when we are away from our Bibles. If we memorize a passage, we can do this easily. "But how does the law get *in your mouth?*" Dallas Willard asked. "By memorization, of course. It becomes an essential part of how we think about everything else as we *dwell on it.*" We come to know it by heart.

We can also do this if in our prayerful reading we have settled on bite-sized segments. The psalms have been a prime place to meditate; one reason is that the images in them (lightning, snarling dogs, broken arms, butter, honey) tend to lodge in our memory easily. Another is that they can be received in small pieces. The image of growling/gnawing calls us to engage fully with the process of meditation. It invites us to read the text aloud, to sing it, to say it with the cadence of our breathing, to connect it to our walking—to experience it as fully as we can.

It can be helpful to think of meditation as what sits on top of our study. In study we look at the meaning of the text. In meditation we seek to have the text and its meaning sink into us. The affections of our heart are reprogrammed. While reading generally takes longer passages of Scripture, our mediation takes smaller portions. Meditation is letting the word do its work on our soul as we deeply hear the word of God in a spirit of surrender. As Dietrich Bonhoeffer wrote, "We want in any case to rise up from our meditation in a different state from when we sat down. We want to meet Christ in his Word. We turn to the text in our desire to hear what it is that he wants to give us and teach us today through his Word."

Meditation is not done well because we follow a precise method. It is done well when we permit the word to seep into our heart, when we drop our guard and allow God to act on us by his living and active word. We recommend that you slow down, take it in and take it away.

SLOW DOWN

An open presence before God cannot be forced, but it can be encouraged. And it is often encouraged when we slow down. Consider for a moment when you are most present with a dear friend. Perhaps you sit on a porch swing. Perhaps you sip a cup of coffee. There are pauses as you think about what the other has just said. Ask yourself, "When have I felt really listened to? When have I really listened?" Often this happens when we set aside our need to "get something done" and give ourselves permission to slow down. The same is true with Scripture meditation.

Hinneh, "I am here," is the word where meditation begins. This was the response of Abraham before the Lord, the response of the boy Samuel when God spoke to him at night in the tabernacle and that of Isaiah when he was undone by the vision of God's holiness. So, you relax and say, "Hinneh, I am here," as you sit to receive the word of life.

We must also come to meditation with the knowledge that we are cherished by God. Without a deeply lived sense of our being God's beloved, we can find the Scriptures to be too threatening. You will have the courage to hear the hard word only when you know it is spoken for your good by One who cherishes you. As you will discover in the following chapter, an attitude of receptive prayer is the house that lectio divina inhabits. "I am here" pervades the entire meditation process. You enter meditation with a prayerful heart. The act of reading and reflecting is an act of prayer. You pause prayerfully after reading to see where the Lord has been present through the Scriptures.

So how can you encourage yourself to slow down for meditation? How can you foster an environment of leisurely presence with God in the Scriptures? It will be different for each person or group. Perhaps you will need to turn off your phone, to retire to a special place at a special time. Perhaps you will want to read the text slowly and appreciatively. Perhaps you will want to begin your time of meditation with some prayerful preparation. Take a few minutes to pray the Lord's Prayer or a favorite psalm, and see if your heart is inclined to the task.

Just as placing a hand in warm water seems to warm the whole body, so a little conscious attention to the Spirit at the onset of prayer can encourage our openness to God throughout our time of meditation. Remember that meditation is a *spiritual* activity. Begin with a simple prayer, asking to be aware of God's presence and for the Spirit to teach you how to meditate. Without making it a spiritual practice, meditation can become a mere reflection on principles or a pursuit of experiences, rather than an encounter with the One who loves you through his love letter for you.

TAKE IT IN

A second aspect of Scripture meditation is the actual "taking it in." In reading we bring the word *to* us. In meditation we receive the word *in* us. And once again, this process will look different for different people.

One of the primary features of Scripture meditation is repetition. We gnaw on it; we regurgitate it; we linger over it; we ponder it again and again. Luther tells his readers to repeat the words of Scripture, "reading and rereading them with diligent attention and reflection, so that you may see what the Holy Spirit means by them. And take care that you do not grow weary or think that you have done enough when you have read, heard, and spoken them once or twice."

Another way we take the Scriptures into us is through the active engagement of our mind and heart and body with the text. We recite a psalm, kneeling, lifting our hands or shouting as the text suggests, trying to understand through our bodies the expression of God's word. We read a story from a Gospel and imagine the scene as if we were watching a movie or reading a novel. Imaginative reflection links thought and emotion to catch what the human authors of

Scripture were seeking to communicate to their readers through their narratives. Similarly we actively engage our feelings as we read poetry or prophecy, trying to capture the mood communicated through the text.

Try reading Scripture as a bodily activity. The fact of the matter is, if meditation is just left as a "mind game," its effects are minimized. Be intentional as you can about your posture and the location of your meditation. At a minimum, adopt a respectful posture that is open—uncross your legs and open your palms to symbolize with your body a receptivity to the work of the Holy Spirit through the text. It was written to be understood by the whole person—heart, mind, soul and strength—so it is good to meditate with the whole person.

Consequently, we also engage our minds. Indeed, the term *meditate* often means simply to "think about" something. Author Simon Tugwell writes of the early Dominicans that "in typical Dominican writers meditation and contemplation retain a straightforwardly intellectual connotation, and they are related far more to ordinary uses of the mind than they are to exercises of piety."

One way to engage our mind with a passage of Scripture is to ask questions. What is going on in this text? What is there to receive from the passage? Is this a text in which God extends a blessing or a promise? Does God extend a command or a warning or a word of love? What should I praise God for? What should I confess?

Do I see any examples to follow? What should I pray for on the basis of this verse? Sometimes meditation requires focus on a particular story, phrase or idea. At other times meditation is an exercise in sacred musing, allowing the mind to wander hither and thither, creatively exploring the connections between text and life.

By meditating on Scripture, we receive the breadth of communication intended by a passage. Remember when you were moved deeply by a speaker. The speaker's message and her passion for the topic and her compelling life story all lined up in a way that moved you. The Greek philosopher Aristotle set forth a theory of persuasion that distinguishes three components: the message (logos), the emotion or force (pathos) and the credibility (ethos). When we read a biblical text, we first are drawn to the words, but unless we attend to how the message is delivered (the pathos and ethos), we may not receive the text as a divine speech-act directed to us. When we sit with the text and come to perceive the author's care and credibility, we are prepared to receive the text more fully.

You can also pay attention to the questions the Scripture asks directly of you. Perhaps you are reading the story of the healing of Bartimaeus (see Mk 10:46-52) and you discover Jesus' question to him: "What do you want me to do for you?" Or you are confronted by Jesus' question to his disciples, "Who do you say that I am?" (Mt 16:15). These questions are intended to do more than request information. They are meant to confront the hearer, to *act*. Furthermore, they are in this written text not merely to record Jesus' questions to his contemporaries, but to address *us* the readers. So, how is God acting toward *you* in these questions? They contain an invitation to express our need to the One who desires our wholeness.

We must see that Scripture is more than invitation; it is a way that God directly acts through his word. The Bible is full of mysteries, and allowing these mysteries to probe our hearts is a good way to take the Scriptures into our lives. Indeed, the perplexities of Scripture and of faith—pressing themselves into our minds and hearts—can at times be profitably understood as an invitation by God to permit his action in our lives.

TAKE IT WITH YOU

After you have taken it in, you will want to keep it with you. You might want to end your time with a particular prayer. Pause and offer a prayer of thanks for the opportunity to sit in God's presence with his word on your lap. Ask what you should take with you into the day ahead. Spiritual writer Madame Guyon (1648-1717) spoke of ending a time of meditation by plucking a "spiritual nosegay" (a fragrant corsage) from the text to carry and refresh oneself periodically through the day. For example, you might want to write a verse on a card to put in your pocket and to read here and there through the day. Others establish times like lunch and dinner to review and ponder a portion. Find your own simple way to take the Scripture with you. Remember the call of Psalm 1 to meditate day and night. This is what we are trying to build in our lives. Generally a through-the-day focus on Scripture comes only when we plan to do it and follow through on that plan.

We also take the word with us when we preach to ourselves the truth we have discovered in the Scripture. Martyn Lloyd-Jones captured the essence of meditation turning into affective prayer: "Have you realized that most of your unhappiness in life is due to the fact that you are listening to yourself instead of talking to yourself?" Learning to speak out for yourself the truth that you have received is transforming in a gracious and life-giving way.

Remember that meditation is about taking it *in you* and *with you*. The meaning you receive from meditation may have relevance for others, but often it has special relevance for you personally (as an individual or as a group doing Scripture meditation together). Through mulling over the text, we often discover both comforting and challenging connections with life. Be on the lookout for these life-connections. Perhaps the passage speaks to you of a relationship you are dealing with. Perhaps the text speaks of an injustice you face. Perhaps you have been touched in some way through the text. Where does the text meet life? The life connections of meditation are very important; they contribute much to the fostering of a sacred life growing from lectio divina. See if there was any call to action from the meditation. If so, make plans to do it. It is important to do what is impressed on you in meditation, or your heart may begin to harden.

There are many other practices that can facilitate meditation. Some find it helpful to set a timer and then let the Scripture tumble in their mind, like clothes in a dryer. With a timer set for five minutes to start, you can confidently begin by telling God you are sitting before him with the passage, ready to hear him speak and to receive his action until the time is up. The timer keeps you from constantly asking, "Have I done this long enough?"

Similarly, it is helpful to have a strategy for dealing with wandering thoughts that arise and pull you away from your meditation. This should not surprise us, for through the centuries Christians have written and discussed the problem of unwanted thoughts. For ordinary thoughts like "remember the milk" or "call Mom," it is a good idea to go into prayer and meditation with a pad of paper nearby. Just write these down, and they will fade away. Negative thoughts are more difficult though. We suggest that when you find that your mind has wandered, simply redirect it—with no self-condemnation—to the Bible passage. It is important that you are gentle with yourself. You are sitting before God in this meditation; trust him to guide and correct. Your job is just to get back to your spiritual work as quickly as you can.

Over the centuries, many Christians have found it helpful to pay attention to their breath—and the God who gives them breath—for a few breaths as part of their meditation (for example, before going back to the text). The wisdom of this comes from the nature of habit formation. Your breath will always be there, whereas the flow and topic of your meditative activity will always be changing. So if you have trained yourself to return to your breath when you are interrupted, you can focus on your breath, which is stable, and from there go back and pick up your meditation. The breath is a marvelous anchor point.

Some people may be surprised at the mention of attending to breath. Yet it is a perfectly natural activity. We alter our breath many times each day in response to different situations: when we exert ourselves climbing stairs, when we are frightened, when there is a sudden change in temperature or when we calm ourselves down. Some of these changes in breathing are below the conscious level of awareness, yet even in these we are still paying attention to our breath. And for some—especially athletes—attention to our breath is practiced consciously.

We can employ our breath as a calming strategy and as a simple way of enhancing our meditative awareness of God. Since the early centuries of Christianity, writers have suggested that paying attention to our breath can be way of becoming more present to God. Why is this? First, paying attention to your breath has a wonderful ability to take you out of your thoughts and schemes and worries to the present moment, and it is in the present moment that we meet God.

Second, in Scripture there is a strong connection between the Spirit and the breath. Both the Hebrew and the Greek words for Spirit have a primary meaning of "breath." This spirit-breath connection was enacted when Jesus gave the Holy Spirit to his disciples: "He breathed on them and said to them, 'Receive the Holy Spirit'" (Jn 20:22). As our lungs fill with air, so we can, as it were, take in the Spirit, and Paul urges his readers, "be filled with the Spirit" (Eph 5:18).

Third, our life is a gift of God. For the writers of Scripture, each breath is seen to be a gift from God. For example, "The spirit of God has made me, and the breath of the Almighty gives me life" (Job 33:4). Just pausing and noticing three breaths can make us aware of life—the life first given when the "LORD God formed man from the dust of the ground, and breathed into his nostrils the breath of life" (Gen 2:7).

So when your thoughts wander in lectio, do not scold or berate yourself; just begin to notice your breath. Perhaps you can say to yourself as you take a few breaths, "Here I am, alive. God has given me life. God's Spirit is with me." Then, from this simple anchor point in reality, return to your practice of Scripture meditation.

We began this chapter by talking about the automatic meditations of the heart, like worry—the way our minds replay past hurts, nurse lusts or toy with fears. Through intentional meditation on Scripture, we begin to reduce the power of the automatic negative thoughts. Meditating on the truth of Scripture works a healing in our being—the promises, hopes and truths of Scripture work their way into our being—and we develop a habit of turning to life-giving thoughts of truth rather than to thoughts that are unhealthy. In this way we benefit from the *content* of our Scripture meditation. But we also benefit from the *process* of meditation. For example, as we learn to focus on Scripture, we gradually develop the skills of ignoring those automatic thoughts we do not desire and instead placing our focus on what we do want to think about.

It makes all the difference what we think we will find in a book when we open its covers. Are we looking for a recipe, a beautiful poem or directions to a museum? Books contain certain things, and it does no good to demand that a given book produce something that is not there.

The psalmist speaks of the word as "gold, even much fine gold" (Ps 19:10). Perhaps people do not receive from the Bible because they look for the wrong thing. Perhaps they do not stick with it long enough to get what is valuable. Mining for gold requires effort. This is the difference between merely reading and meditating. Oh, that we would give God's word the leisure of whole-hearted meditation!

6

PRAYING

Phoebe Palmer was desperate. It was July 29, 1836. The nurse assigned with the duties of caring for her infant daughter had carelessly lit a lamp near the child's crib curtain, and it caught fire. The nurse shrieked, and Phoebe ran to find her child enveloped in flames. She grasped her darling from the blaze, but the child soon breathed her last. Phoebe, turning away from others, retired to her room to be with God. She later recounted,

> In the agony of my soul, I had exclaimed, "O what shall I do!" And the answer now came,—"Be still and know that I am God." I took up the precious WORD, and cried, "O teach me the lesson of this trial," and the first lines to catch my eye on opening the Bible, were these, "O, the depth of the riches, both of the wisdom and knowledge of God! how unsearchable are his judgments and his ways past finding out!"

This divine guidance would trigger for her a very momentous year of reassessment, one that would set the foundations in place to make her an effective and influential Christian leader.

What is prayer? Phoebe Palmer's cry for help was a prayer of request. The term *pray* often is connected with ordinary requests. In civil lawsuits, the plaintiff expresses a request for a judgment in what is known as the "prayer for relief." Similarly we pray as Christians, expressing a range of petitions to God. Yet in another sense, prayer involves more than just petition making.

Paul spoke of "all kinds of prayer" in Ephesians 6:18 (NIV) and mentioned specifically "supplications, prayers, intercessions, and thanksgivings" made in reference to government officials (1 Tim 2:1). Jesus, when asked to teach his disciples to pray, offered them a model of prayer that included worship, surrender, petition, confession and cries for deliverance (see Lk 11:2-4). And the psalms, of course, express everything from contented rest (Ps 131) to uninhibited praise (Ps 100) to angry complaint (Ps 13). Indeed, Christian prayer communicates every aspect and mood of human life.

And that is the point. Prayer is simply communication with God, speaking, listening and the space-in-between. Just as communication between humans involves gestures, moods, tone of voice, waiting, our sense of the current state of the relationship and so on, so our communication with the personal God involves a similar collection of elements. We may speak to God before opening Scripture, asking for the Spirit's illumination. We may listen to the Spirit before opening Scripture, waiting for a sense of where to read. We may speak to God with a phrase from the text. We may hesitate as we read, aware of the tension of our relationship with God concerning an issue addressed in a passage. We may wait silently with a phrase of the text, attending to the loving space-in-between our listening and speech. Prayer is the relational place within which our interaction with Scripture is performed, whether we are a simpleton, a skeptic or a scholar.

In times of crisis, we—like Phoebe—cry out in prayer and turn to Scripture. Prayer and Scripture—they are wed together again and again. The old adage that "in prayer we speak to God and in Scripture we listen to God" describes in simplest terms how important these two are together in our communication with God. Reading, meditation and prayer are also often linked as a natural progression. Historian Charles Hambrick-Stowe, for example, described American Puritan practice in this way:

> In the practice of secret devotion—especially in the early morning, at night just prior to sleep, at midday on the Sabbath or days of fasting, and on Saturday in preparation for the Sabbath—individuals ideally meditated after reading and before prayer. Meditation was the natural outcome of reading in that the substance of the exercise often emerged from the passage read. In meditation, the

believer applied the written test to the soul. Meditation was linked with prayer, since the saint then slipped inevitably into conversation with God.

Yet while it is simple and natural to think of prayer and its relationship with meditation and Scripture in such ways, we suggest that both lectio divina and the rich diversity of prayer are best understood when we see prayer as not merely one half of a dialogue or one moment in a progression, but rather as intimately connected with every moment of our devotional reading of Scripture—before, during and after—and indeed as the "house" lectio divina inhabits. But to see prayer in this way, we must briefly consider just what prayer *is*.

PRAYER BEFORE READING AND MEDITATING

Perhaps the most obvious connection between prayer and reading or meditating is the simple cry for assistance prior to opening the text. Phoebe Palmer, in her despair, went to open her Bible and pleaded for God's help in her time of need. But we also need help even in the act of understanding the text we open to read. Consequently Martin Luther suggested that prayer is the leading step of good theology. He wrote,

Firstly, you should know that the Holy Scriptures constitute a book which turns the wisdom of all other books into foolishness, because not one teaches about eternal life except this one alone. Therefore you should straightway despair of your reason and understanding.... But kneel down in your little room and pray to God with real humility and earnestness, that he through his dear Son may give you his Holy Spirit, who will enlighten you, lead you, and give you understanding.

While it is certainly valuable to lift up a request for the Spirit's illumination prior to a time of reading and meditating on Scripture, we suggest that you go one step further. Use this moment before reading as an occasion for laying yourself before God, admitting/confessing who you are as you approach this text and asking for the particular kinds of guidance you know you need as you open the Scriptures.

We learned in chapter three that we often come to God (and Scripture) with a divided heart, with minds more conformed to the world than to God. Yet the various ways we all conform to the world shape the way we read Scripture. They all influence "what we see" in the text. Consequently, it is wise, right at the front of our devotional reading, to present our viewpoints, circumstances and questions honestly before the Lord and the text, open for the "I" who reads the text to be transformed by it.

For example, I glance at my reading/meditation passage for the day and realize it is a prophet's declaration of God's judgment of Israel. Perhaps I've read a couple of passages like this before, and I don't really "get it." In fact, God appeared to me to be cruel in those passages. So today I begin my devotional time with a prayer like this: "O God, I know that you are God, the Creator of everything. You are the One whose story is told in this book and whose Spirit helps me to understand it. But when I hear about what you intend to do in your judgments, I don't like it. It bothers me. You know that I experienced horrible violence during the war. And people called it God's judgment. Maybe I just don't understand. It's not that I am using this issue as an excuse not to believe—or follow—you. I really want to understand you. Teach me how the portrait of you in this passage relates to other passages that speak so much of your love and forgiveness. I know that you may show me here and now, or that it may take some time and lots of reading and meditating. Amen." In this kind of prayer before reading, the fullness of our communication with God—speaking, listening and the space-in-between—is laid open before God right from the start.

PRAYER DURING READING AND MEDITATING

Prayer also arises in the midst of our reading and meditating. Imagine yourself reading along in the first chapter of I Timothy. You read about Paul's transformation in Christ, and then in verse 17 you bump into this: "To the King of the ages, immortal, invisible, the only God, be honor and glory forever and ever. Amen." Or you are reading along through the prophecies of Jeremiah, and you come to the first verse of chapter twelve: "You will be in the right, O Lord, when I lay charges against you; but let me put my case before you." Or you are starting Paul's letter to the Philippians, and you hear Paul pray in verse nine "that your love may overflow more and more with knowledge and full insight."

There are many, many places in the Scripture that are prayers themselves. It is only natural that we would take these prayers and offer them up to God as our own prayers. "O Lord," you might pray, having read the passage in Philippians, "I ask that the love of my friends who volunteer at the soup kitchen will overflow more and more. They told me on Sunday that it has been a hard week there—a fight even broke out one day. Give them an overflowing love in the midst of this, God. Let their love overflow with knowledge and insight. Give them the wisdom to handle these situations when they get out of hand. Help them see into the hearts of the people they work with, and help them to really *know* the people who come to them for food. Amen."

As Benedictine Archbishop Mariano Magrassi put it, "All we need to do is read, listen, and ruminate. Then, having filled those words with all our thought, our love, and our life, we repeat to God what he has said to us. The Word is not only the center of our listening; it is also the center of our response."

Even passages that are not actually prayers can be reworded into prayers of many kinds. You might take, for example, the Beatitudes in Matthew 5:6-9 and make them into a collection of requests, confessions and thanksgivings: "O God, sometimes I really do hunger and thirst for righteousness, both in my own life and in the world more generally. I thank you that you have birthed this longing in my heart, even though at times I actually feel this thirst as a kind of pain or sorrow over things that aren't the way you want them. In fact, at times I get bitter and judgmental, even though you say in the next verse that it is 'the merciful who are blessed.' I want to be pure in heart, Lord, I really do. Fill me with your Spirit so I am more controlled by you than by my own impure heart. Oh, and about peacemaking, Father, I am so thankful for the opportunity to help that couple yesterday who were at odds. It seemed like good things happened for them. I don't get many opportunities to be a peacemaker, but it sure feels good. As I remember that encounter, I feel you calling me a child of God. Amen."

In all kinds of ways, we can use the language of Scripture to help us form our own speech to God. As Edward Bickersteth suggested, "Christians would find no small advantage by constantly turning what they read into prayer or praise; for hereby the instruction of the Bible would be more confirmed in their minds, and their hearts would be more engaged in the practice of them."

Not only our speech to God but also our listening and the experience of our spaces between the listening and speaking can be shaped by our reading of the text, even during the act of reading. You are reading the story of Peter walking on water, and you pause mid-story. Jesus says, "Why did you doubt?" You feel something inside, some kind of nudge in your spirit. The phrase speaks to you. You listen to it again, only this time with a slight change of emphasis: "Why do *you* doubt?" Then you sit with the phrase, perhaps reflecting on the history and character of your own doubt, until the feeling lifts. Perhaps only a minute or two. Perhaps much longer. Then you go back to the verse and begin reading where you left off.

Another way we can listen to God's voice in the text as we read is to employ the active use of our minds, hearts, bodies and imaginations, as we mentioned in the chapter on meditation.

We hear different nuances of the Spirit when we formally outline the structure of Paul's arguments in Romans, or when we imaginatively picture the excitement around Josiah's discovery of the law in 2 Kings 22, or when we recite a psalm with both body and voice. It is not just a matter of reading or studying or praying the text. The point is that we actually notice—we *hear*—different aspects of the voice of the divine Author by using these different ways of interacting with the Scripture.

We could give many more examples of ways that reading the Scriptures and praying the Scriptures go hand in hand. We speak to God with the language of Scripture. We hear the Spirit of God through the text. We sense our presence to God and God's presence to us alive and growing, even as we interact with Scripture. Our hope is that with these few suggestions, you can figure out how to experiment with your own ideas. We are sure that God will be delighted.

PRAYER AFTER READING AND MEDITATING

Prayer is not only a way of being present to God at the onset or during our sacred reading, it also flows naturally out of the act of reading and meditating on Scripture. We heard Philip Doddridge in chapter four urge us, "If you pray over the substance of this Scripture with your Bible open before you, it may impress your memory and your heart yet more deeply, and may form you to a copiousness and variety, both of thought and expression, in prayer." What we read, and what we consider and experience in meditation, issues forth in prayer.

One way that our prayers follow our reading and meditation is that, inspired by something in the text, we find ourselves praying for God to guide us regarding how to obey what we hear in the text and how to follow where we are led by the text. Medieval scholar Hugh of St. Victor (d. 1142), for example, described a progression from reading *(lectio)*, meditation *(meditatio)* and prayer *(oratio)* into action *(operatio)* and finally into contemplation *(contemplatio)*. For Hugh, the function of meditation was to provide wisdom or "counsel" concerning the meaning and significance of Scripture. Prayer, then, provides the link between our understanding of the meaning of Scripture and our active living out of the text. He wrote,

> Further, since the counsel of man is weak and ineffective without divine aid, arouse yourself to prayer and ask the help of him without whom you can accomplish no good thing, so that by his grace, which, going before you has enlightened you, he may guide your feet, as you follow, onto the road of peace; and so that he may bring that which as yet is in your will alone, to concrete effect in good performance.

But prayer after reading is not merely an "asking what to do." It is also the development of the work of God experienced through reading and meditation. Sometimes when we read a text, we are not led to a particular action, but are the recipients of the ministry of the Spirit. We sense a touch of healing, we hear God's voice of love, or we are shaken, challenged by what we read. Prayer in these moments simply gives voice to our experience, advancing it toward contemplative intimacy with God.

Not long after Hugh of St. Victor, Guigo II (d. around 1188) wrote a book entitled *The Ladder of Monks*. Guigo's "ladder" moves from reading through meditating and prayer and is completed in contemplation. Thus for Guigo, prayer serves as the bridge between meditation and contemplation. The longing for God that is birthed in reading and meditation is developed in prayer to be fulfilled in the contemplative vision of God. He prays,

> I seek by reading and meditating what is true purity of heart and how it may be had, so that with its help I may know you, if only a little. Lord, for long have I meditated in my heart, seeking to see your face. It is the sight of you, Lord, that I have sought; and all the while in my meditation the fire of longing, the desire to know you more fully, has increased. When you break for me the bread of sacred Scripture, you have shown yourself to me in that breaking

of bread, and the more I see you, the more I long to see you, no more from without, in the rind of the letter, but within, in the letter's hidden meaning. Nor do I ask this, Lord, because of my own merits, but because of your mercy. I too in my unworthiness confess my sins with the woman who said that "even the little dogs eat of the fragments that fall from the table of their masters." So give me, Lord, some pledge of what I hope to inherit, at least one drop of heavenly rain with which to refresh my thirst, for I am on fire with love.

In your reading and meditation, the Spirit of God may plant a seed. It may be a seed of action, or longing, or sorrow, or healing or something else. You may be part of a sacred reading group or alone in your sacred place. Whether you are an individual or a congregation, you recognize the seed planted. You follow James's direction: "Welcome with meekness the implanted word that has the power to save your souls" (Jas 1:21). The bottom may have dropped out of your life and you are facing the divorce that you could never have imagined, and in the midst of this you read, "How beautiful you are, my love, how very beautiful!" (Song 4:1). You understand the context and it becomes the word spoken to you by God. The word seems implanted. In dark times you turn, and there it is. It is a little ray of light, an assurance. You welcome it with meekness and allow it to reassure you and set you right.

Prayer—after reading and meditation—notices and waters this seed. Who knows what it will become when it grows? The job of prayer is to give voice to what we hear, what we need to speak, what is going on in the space-in-between of our relationship with God. Author Basil Pennington suggests that we select a "word of life" from our reading each day and carry it with us as we go throughout our day with the intent to meditatively repeat it whenever we get the chance. Is this prayer after our time of meditation? Or is this meditating after our time of prayer? Perhaps at these points the labels are unnecessary. What is important is our developing relationship with God through the Scriptures.

PRAYER AS THE HOUSE THAT LECTIO DIVINA INHABITS

Prayer is more than some word we offer before, during or after our Scripture meditation. Prayer—communication with God—is the house that lectio divina inhabits. The materials of this house are rich and varied. Some even seem exotic today. Out of sight, its solid and sure foundation is surrender. Before prayer is words, it is a gesture—a gesture of surrender. "To pray means to open your hands before God," Henri Nouwen wrote. Prayer is born of our perceived helplessness. We open our hands to receive what we lack, and we know it can be received only as a gift. What do these open hands of surrender look like? Four words describe this posture: broken, blessed, receptive and quiet.

Broken. The broken person knows she needs God's grace to live as much as she needs oxygen. An optimistic brokenness—optimistic about the power of grace and wary about our motives and the fickleness of our stick-to-it-ive-ness—is the attitude needed for prayer. Jesus reminds us that unless we die to our sense of competence we will not flourish in his kingdom: "I tell you, unless a grain of wheat falls into the earth and dies, it remains just a single grain; but if it dies, it bears much fruit" (Jn 12:24). Ole Hallesby wrote, "Listen, my friend! Your helplessness is your best prayer." Our weakness, our helplessness, our brokenness, our inability to fix what we really want changed is the essential gesture of prayer. Use the gesture of sitting with open hands to symbolize your neediness as you begin your time of lectio.

Blessed. Jesus' model prayer for Christians begins with the inviting words "Our Father, who art in heaven." We come in our helplessness and we are present as beloved children to our loving Father. Secure in this love and in the certainty of God's blessing, we can "approach the throne of grace with boldness, so that we may receive mercy and find grace to help in time of need" (Heb 4:16). We come to prayer saying, "I am accepted," which reminds us that we are beloved children, not spiritual orphans who need to earn a place at the table.

Receptive. We come with an eager expectation to receive. Our reading and study are marked by deliberation and hard work as we seek to extract the meaning, but underneath all of this must be a gentle, receptive spirit. Like Joseph, we say, "Do not interpretations belong to God?" (Gen 40:8). We wrestle and wonder, but our ear is always cocked in the process to hear God direct us and point out what is most significant for us. As we read we know that "the sacred writings ... have power to make [us] wise and lead [us] to salvation through faith in Christ Jesus" (2 Tim 3:15 NEB). We say, "Speak, for your servant is listening" (1 Sam 3:10) as we begin.

Quiet. Often our minds are abuzz with care and worries. Many people have learned to attend to the automatic negative thinking that courses through their minds, making it impossible for them to hear the affirming word from the Master Affirmer. For "we all must eventually turn to the Master Affirmer, God the Father," Leanne Payne wrote, "for our true identity, our real authentic selves. He heals the unaffirmed by sending His affirming word. And we all must receive this." Isaiah said that this inability to come in quiet left God's people spiritually bereft: "In returning and rest you shall be saved; in quietness and in trust shall be your strength. But you refused" (Is 30:15).

When we speak of quieting our minds, we are not asking you to switch your brains off somehow, but simply to diminish your attention to distractions, worries and negative thinking. This takes training, but two simple methods have helped many people. One is to record things that come to mind during prayer, as we have mentioned. Second, it is helpful to wind down the RPMs of your mind by coming into the present moment. God is found in his word in the present, not in our imaginings and fantasies.

What do we mean by coming into the present moment? Use your body to take you into the present, for example, by walking slowly and prayerfully before you sit. Notice your walking, and as your mind wanders, bring it back gently to the fact of your walking. As we mentioned earlier, you may want to pay attention to your breath, and as thoughts arise, redirect your attention to your breath and then go on with your reading. Don't scold yourself for wandering off; just return. As you begin, take a breath and watch the miracle that it is, affirming that you want to dwell quietly in the present and in the reality of "God with us."

These four gestures open us to prayerful reading and the grace-filled surrender that allows us to attend to Scripture so that it reads us as we read it.

We have spoken of prayer as a receptive activity—a way of being before God, but it also is an active crying out to God, even as part of the house where lectio divina dwells. Consider an image from the book of Revelation. This is one of the most encouraging books in Scripture and one that helps reset our internal compass; it celebrates God's victory and makes heaven and the spiritual so tangible and real. This passage, Revelation 5:6-8, speaks of the greatness of Christ and his redemptive work. It begins the announcement that an important scroll needs to be opened, but no one can be found to open it. John weeps at this news, but is heartened to hear that the lion of the tribe of Judah can open it. He turns to see not a lion but a lamb—a lamb that bears the marks of sacrifice, but one possessed of power and ready for action. Here is the heart of the New Testament: victory through sacrifice.

THE INEVITABLE DISTRACTIONS

Distractions come in our times of quiet prayer. How we deal with these inevitable distractions is more important than the fact of their coming. We suggest that you approach them with curiosity, grace and discipline.

Many people find that being careful about when and where they meditate helps limit distracting thoughts. Try to find a place that can be your "meditation corner." A chair, a quiet path, a train ride—some spot where you do not normally work or daydream. Your body will help you pray if you set aside a space.

After your time of prayer, exercise your *curiosity* about the nature of the distractions. Let yourself look back at your prayer time for a moment. What was your experience of distractions in this time of prayer like? If they consisted mostly of simple to-do items, consider keeping a tablet at hand and then take some time to clear your mind of such things before you meditate. If the thoughts have a particular theme, you might consider seeing how these thoughts might respond to you speaking to them. Consider saying things like, "The worries about my job are real, but it has never helped me to pursue those, so I am going to return to the truth before me." What happens to the thoughts when you simply name them—"That's a lustful thought," "That's a thought of revenge," "That's a negative thought"? By exercising healthy curiosity about our distractions, we can develop strategies to avoid their negative influence.

When thoughts come to you and lead you astray, do not admonish yourself. Extend grace to yourself as you return to the task at hand. Too often we allow our distractions to become fatal to the beginning of our life of prayer. The distractions come, and the sincere pray-er becomes frustrated and chastises himself or herself. Don't allow this to happen. Go forth in faith that God, through habit formation and his healing presence, will quiet the distractions eventually or that he will do his work in spite of your distracted mind.

Finally, we exercise *discipline*. Henri Nouwen aptly captured the wisdom of the desert tradition when he wrote,

Time in solitude may at first seem little more than a time in which we are bombarded by thousands of thoughts and feelings that emerge from hidden areas of our mind. One of the early Christian writers describes the first stage of solitary prayer as the experience of a man who, after years of living with open doors, suddenly decides to shut them. The visitors who used to come and enter his home start pounding on his doors, wondering why they are not allowed to enter. Only when they realize that they are not welcome do they gradually stop coming. This is the experience of anyone who decides to enter into solitude after a life without much spiritual discipline. At first, the many distractions keep presenting themselves. Later, as they receive less and less attention, they slowly withdraw.

Notice what is said about prayer.

> Then I saw between the throne and the four living creatures and among the elders a Lamb standing as if it had been

slaughtered, having seven horns and seven eyes, which are the seven spirits of God sent out into all the earth. He went and took the scroll from the right hand of the one who was seated on the throne. When he had taken the scroll, the four living creatures and the twenty-four elders fell before the Lamb, each holding a harp and golden bowls full of incense, which are the prayers of the saints. (Rev 5:6-8)

We have here an image of prayers being received by God. This image shows the access we have to God through prayer. It shows their value and God's gracious reception of our prayers. First, access. The prayers of God's people entered directly into the power center of the universe—heaven. The image of our prayers going right to the heart of heaven and being personally presented to God should be an encouragement to pray.

Second, value. Gold was the most precious commodity known in biblical times. To capture what this image connotes, all we need to do is paraphrase it: "They were holding plastic grocery bags that contained the prayers of the saints." How precious are your prayers? So precious that they are carried before God in golden bowls. The Greek word points to golden bowls used in religious ceremonies—gold in worship was far beyond the personal experience of these persecuted Christians.

Third, grace. "Golden bowls full of incense." For an ancient Hebrew, incense and worship were bound together. Incense was at the heart of Israelite worship. It was as essential to corporate worship as we would regard singing or prayer. Consider what happened each year on the Day of Atonement. The high priest entered the dimly lit tabernacle with trepidation. In one hand was a censer, hot with glowing coals from the altar. In the other were two handfuls of incense. As he moved behind the curtain into the holy of holies, he put the incense on the coals, producing a fragrant cloud over the ark of the covenant, the footstool of Yahweh. Thus, the place of the Presence was shrouded in aromatic smoke.

For the ancient Hebrew, this is a picture of proper worship. Throughout Scripture, incense is associated with fully consecrated worship and prayer. Incense was expensive and not accessible to members of the persecuted early church. Consider how encouraging it would have been for them to hear, "And the smoke of the incense, with the prayers of the saints, rose before God from the hand of the angel" (Rev 8:4). They offered their prayers in barren places or huddled in homes, but these simple prayers do not simply make it to heaven—they are borne before God in golden bowls and infused with incense by God himself. So this image of incense is a picture of God's grace. Our halting and confused prayers enter heaven enriched by the incense of his love and grace.

As we come to Scripture with a heart of prayer, we have an opportunity to come into God's magnificent throne room and to experience, for a moment, our heart's true home. Prayer is asking, but also so much more. In fact, it is more than words. It is first and foremost a way of life before God, marked by a humble and loving relationship with God. Consequently when reading Scripture in an attitude of prayer, our reading of Scripture becomes simply one more form of intimate communication with God. And this, in turn, results in the transformation of our lives.

7
CONTEMPLATING

Picture that you are talking with someone. What is going on during this conversation? At one level, you are simply talking and listening. There is the forming of words, the hearing and the making sense of the words of the other. At the same time, there is another level of activity going on. At this level you are navigating the conversation in yourself. *What does she think of me? Is that question for real, or is she just trying to get information out of me? I kind of like the way her shoes go with that blouse. I'm gonna have to leave in a few minutes, but I'd really like to get to know her better.* And so on. If you pay careful attention to a conversation, you can actually be aware of both levels active in yourself at the same time.

But there is also a third level. Beneath the words, beneath the questions and the posturing, there is simply you, present to this person, and this person present to you. Can you feel it? All the thoughts and words and such lie on top of your simple and fundamental presence to each other. In any conversation, this third level has its own character, just as the other two levels have their own. When the other is a stranger, you are "present" in a different way than when the other is a close friend. The same question asked at the second level ("What does she think of me?") feels different when you are present to a friend or a stranger. Your mood, the state of your relationship and more all influence the quality of this subtle presence to another. And if you are very attentive, you can actually be aware of *all three* levels of communication at the same time.

Sometimes the richest moments of a relationship are when you are able to dwell in this third level. We offer comfort to a child by scooping him up and holding him while he wails after a tumble. We hold a friend while she cries on our shoulder and between the sobs tells of her father's death and her pain at being halfway across the country when it happened. We speak no words, but offer the deep gift of being present. And that person senses the comfort of being deeply understood.

Now let's change the image. Instead of imagining yourself talking to someone, imagine yourself reading the Scriptures. Now what is going on?

Well, there is the first layer, right? You are reading the letters, forming words and sentences in your mind or with your mouth (if you are reading aloud). At the same time, the second level is going on: the questions and ideas as you navigate the text. *I've read this text before. That is a really strange comment; I never understood that.*

I like the way the words flow from this verse to the next. Is that verse talking about me? and so on.

But underneath the words, underneath the questions and responses, just as in human-to-human relationships, silently grounding the very character of the experience of Scripture reading itself, is your simple presence to God and God's presence to you. Your unconfessed sins, your spiritual hopes, your desire to be held in the midst of your pain—the state of your relationship with God—is there, right there, every time you open the Bible to read. Just as mutual presence is the ground of any human interaction, so mutual presence is the hidden ground of lectio divina. And if you pay careful attention, you can be aware of this third level.

So, before you read, or underneath your meditation, or flowing from your prayer, there is presence. Christian contemplation is the intuition or awareness of the presence of God; it's being mindful of the presence of God. That is why it is good to begin a time of lectio with a simple acknowledgement that you know you are in the presence of God. We are slowly remade just from the intentional exposure to God's heart of love.

When we *meditate*, we reflect; we gnaw on the text a bit. We take it into us by actively employing our thoughts and feelings. When we *pray* we communicate with God: asking for wisdom, listening for God's voice, speaking back what comes to mind. When we *contemplate* during lectio divina, we rest, present with the God of the text.

We are simply present with God, and God completes the work. What happens in contemplation is God's grace. Gregory the Great of Rome (c. 540-604), after reflecting on the public ministry of Scripture, described something of the grace of the Lord when a soul privately reflects on Scripture:

> Through the grace of the Lord Almighty it often happens that certain things in scripture are better understood when God's word is read in private. The soul, conscious of its faults when it recognizes what it hears, pierces itself with the dart of pain and transfixes itself with the sword of compunction so that it can do nothing but weep.... In the midst of this, the soul is at times taken up to contemplate sublime things, the desire for which tortures it with a sweet weeping.

In the midst of our reading, meditation and prayer, the Spirit moves. And at times we are taken up to "contemplate" sublime things (echoing Rev 4:1-2).

Another person who was taken up to contemplate divine things was Puritan minister Cotton Mather (1663-1728). He wrote in his diary about a time when, while using his typical methods of devotion (which included Scripture reading, meditation and prayer), "heaven has come near to me, and filled me with joy unspeakable and full of glory. I cannot utter, I may not utter, the Communications of heaven, whereto this day I have been this day admitted: but this I will say, *I have tasted that the Lord is gracious.*"

For both Gregory and Mather, contemplation has an element of passive reception (of *grace*) to it. Contemplation is not something we *do*. It is rather something we *experience*. Whether accompanied by joys unspeakable, a shattering conviction, a simple calm or very little at all, *contemplation* refers to the experienced encounter between one person (God) present to another.

THE WORD CONTEMPLATION

The fact of the matter is that the term *contemplation* has a long and complicated history. Different individuals and groups have used this term to mean different things. Gregory the Great understood contemplation as an experience of seeing the divine. Ignatius of Loyola used the term to describe a form of Gospel meditation. To some, *contemplation* was a synonym of *meditation* and simply meant "thinking about," while other Christians identified contemplation with emotional experiences of the sweetness of God. Still further distinctions were developed between "active" contemplation (seen as the result of disciplined attending to God) and "infused" contemplation (understood as a supernatural gift whereby the recipient becomes totally centered on God). The term *contemplation* can be used to describe a way of doing prayer, an attitude that permeates our prayer or an aim of prayer.

Even though the term has been used to mean different things throughout history, contemplation has been identified for many centuries as a significant element of lectio divina. John Smaragdus of St. Mihiel (d. after 825) distinguished between prayer *(oratio)*, which communicates a desire for God kindled through the reading and meditation of Scripture, and contemplation *(contemplatio)*, which is the goal of the desire, a beginning of the joys of eternity. What prayer seeks, contemplation finds. In the twelfth century, Guigo II interpreted the elements of lectio divina as a model of different stages of life: progressing from meditation to prayer and finally to contemplation, which was the fulfillment of the Christian life.

More recently, Cistercian abbot and author Thomas Keating described the interplay of meditation, prayer and contemplation in terms of two "parts" of human experience: the reflective part and the will:

> The reflective part, pondering upon the words of the sacred text was called meditatio, "meditation." The spontaneous movement of the will in response to these reflections was called oratio, "affective prayer." Affective in the sense of one's deepest desires. Here our focus shifts subtly

from the mind, as in reading, to the will. And as these reflections and our repenting and resolving become more centered, one moved on to a state of resting in the presence of God, and that is what was meant by contemplatio, "contemplation."

Keating's understanding of this dynamic movement of thought and will—and the centering of these in the contemplative experience of the presence of God—is a foundation stone of his approach to what is now commonly called "centering prayer."

In this chapter we will explore contemplation as a resting in God and an enjoyment of the pleasure of his company. More particularly, we will look at contemplation with reference to three features: presence, silence and love.

GOD'S PRESENCE

Contemplation is about being with God. Behind the words, the thoughts, the anxious feelings and the distractions, underneath all the activities of lectio divina, we are right there, present with God. And God is present with us. God is always present with us, and God is especially present to us in Scripture.

God is beholding you right now: "For the eyes of the LORD range throughout the entire earth" (2 Chron 16:8-9). "'Who can hide in secret places so that I cannot see them?' says the LORD. 'Do not I fill heaven and earth?' says the LORD" (Jer 23:24). Throughout the day, God is gazing at you. "His eye is on the sparrow, and I know he watches me," as the old hymn says. Theologically we refer to this as God's omnipresence—he is present everywhere (everything is present to God) and is cognizant of all creation. Throughout Scripture we are told that God is present—that we cannot escape his presence. "Where can I go from your spirit?" the psalmist asked. "Where can I flee from your presence?" (Ps 139:7). The omnipresence of God is the foundation of contemplation. Through contemplative prayer we learn to pay attention to God's presence anywhere and everywhere.

Orthodox bishop Anthony Bloom tells a delightful story in his classic book, *Beginning to Pray*. An old lady came to him with a concern when he was a young priest. She had been praying the prescribed prayers of the church for many years, but as she put it, "Never have I perceived God's presence at all." And so Bloom gave her some advice. She was to sit in her armchair after breakfast; she was to look around her room and see what was there; she was to light a little lamp before her icon of Christ; and then she was to take up her knitting and knit before the face of God for fifteen minutes.

"But," Bloom commanded, "I forbid you to say one word of prayer. You just knit and try to enjoy the peace of your room." She obeyed the priest's instructions and was surprised to discover the smallest noises, and then a rich silence. And then, "all of a sudden," the lady reported, "I perceived that the silence was a presence. At the heart of the silence there was He who is all stillness." God's presence can be found anywhere if we only permit ourselves to find it.

Yet it is also appropriate to speak of God's presence and ministry to us as being perceived more concretely. God is present to us through the sacraments, through the work of the Holy Spirit and through the gifts of the body of Christ. More particularly to our point in this book, God is also present to us through the Scriptures. In some way, God is especially and effectively present through the word (Is 55:10-11 and Heb 4:12 speak of this). We invest ourselves in lectio divina, expecting to encounter God, precisely because it is *divina;* because, with John Calvin "we feel a divine energy living in it [the Bible]—an energy by which we are drawn and animated to obey it."

We count on the illumination of Scripture: the Holy Spirit whispering, explaining God's love letter to us and impressing on us its importance. The presence of God is mediated through the word of God. The word of God is comprehended through the assistance of the Spirit of God. Contemplative reading, then, is an approach to the text of Scripture that pays special attention—beneath the mere analysis of words and questions—to the dynamics of our presence to God and God's presence to us through the Spirit. It's just like the elderly woman, but instead of knitting in front of a picture of Jesus, we are leisurely reading a book: *The Book*.

SILENCE

Reading, meditating and praying make much use of human activities (thinking, imagination, emotion, words, postures and so on). When we are contemplating, however, we tend to withdraw from our words and imaginations and such, preferring simply to rest with God. Contemplation is comfortable with silence. If, as we have learned, presence lies underneath speech and mental activities, it is helpful, especially at first, to pay attention to God's presence in an environment of silence. This is why "contemplatives" are often thought of as quiet and solitary people.

The prelude to the Lord's Prayer in the Sermon on the Mount has long been seen as a valuable teaching on silence. Jesus advises that when we are praying we should "not heap up empty phrases as the Gentiles do; for they think that they will be heard because of their many words. Do not be like them, for your Father knows what you need before you ask him" (Mt 6:7-8). Why does Jesus command us to shun wordiness in prayer? Through words we exercise our dominion over many areas of our life, and in stepping back from words, we acknowledge

God's rightful place and surrender our desire to control. As Orthodox bishop Kallistos Ware wrote, "To achieve silence: this is of all things the hardest and the most decisive in the art of prayer. Silence is not merely negative—a pause between words, a temporary cessation of speech—but, properly understood, it is highly positive: an attitude of attentive alertness, of vigilance, and above all of listening."

Silence can be part of the physical atmosphere we structure into our time of lectio. Silence may also arise spontaneously in the midst of our practice of lectio. We read a passage, and our thoughts drift gently into contemplative rest. They are not necessarily gone, but quiet, as we sit with what we read and with the One who is present as we read. However, the silence we experience might not be a tranquil rest at all. We may read and meditate and pray, and be drawn bit by bit through the text into a face-to-face confrontation with the living God. We are undone, as Isaiah exclaimed, and our only response is to stand mute before our Maker (Is 6).

Silence is also a condition of heart. To cultivate heart-silence is to learn to still (or to just ignore) the chatter and preoccupying thoughts and feelings that plague us when we sit still. Inner silence means not necessarily expecting any particular encounters with of God. It means resting, waiting before God, who brings what he will bring. Contemplative silence is not some spiritual achievement, but is rather a way of surrender and a practice that develops over time. A contemplative approach assumes that our perception of any particular experience will fall short of the infinite divinity we know as God.

On the one hand, in contemplation we are comfortable with or without spiritual experiences, content to rest even in the midst of "holy boredom." And yet having said this, it is also fair to say that the prayer of tongues can be considered a contemplative experience, an encounter in which ordinary language and concepts are transcended. The apostle Paul tells us, "If I pray in a tongue, my spirit prays but my mind is unproductive" (1 Cor 14:14). One cannot be too dogmatic when dealing with the mysterious presence of the living God.

Through the centuries, Christians have made much of Elijah's encounter with God. He did not hear him in "the wind; and after the wind an earthquake, but the LORD was not in the earthquake; and after the earthquake a fire, but the LORD was not in the fire," but he heard him in "a sound of sheer silence" (1 Kings 19:11-12). That God comes in silence and that his Spirit is depicted as a dove, a bird that is easily chased away, told these Christians of the need to learn to be quiet and discerningly open.

If our practice of lectio divina is going to have any contemplative dimension, we will have to get used to a certain amount of silence. In contemplation we take our hands off the steering wheel and leave the controls to God. In all the phases of lectio divina, there is always the presence of human initiative (we read with care and analysis, we repeat a phrase, we offer up our bewilderment in prayer), and there is divine initiative (God gives us his word to read, God acts toward us through his word, God calls us to pray). But in contemplation our initiative is surrender—we can only await God's action toward us.

Contemplation is a bit like bird watching; we can't make the birds show up, but there are things we can do to encourage them. Likewise, there are things we can do to signal a mellowness of heart and an interest in doing business with God. We open our Bible. We make a habit of stilling our speech for a while. We wait in our silence for the silence of God to come. But in the end, God just comes.

The point is, in contemplation we must be ready for all kinds of silence. In contemplation we seek simply to cultivate a disciplined silence that reflects a focused and listening stance. And in this sense, contemplation is not only about presence, it is also about absence. Christian contemplative silence is a space between places, where, trusting in our justification and the love of God, we expose ourselves and open ourselves to change. In lectio divina, this change process is guided by the Scriptures. It is a space of vulnerability and openness, an emptiness that arises from the loving presence of God and feeds our loving knowledge of God.

LOVE

Let us return once again to our imagination of a conversation. As you recall that third level—the level of presence to one another—you notice that there is a particular character to your presence toward others. You notice that it is different for a stranger and a friend, and even during different moments. What you are noticing is the state of the relationship within a slice of life. You can see the factors that make the relationship *what it is* at that time. You can feel the harmonies or tensions that shape the character of your presence. What you are aware of is the state of the "union" of your relationship. You are attending to your love, the dynamics of your interest, connection, self-giving and more. The same is true in the contemplative dimension of devotional reading. As we contemplate Scripture, we become conscious of our union with God in love.

First, there is God's love for us. Jesus said, "I give you a new commandment, that you love one another. Just as I have loved you, you also should love one another. By this everyone will know that you are my disciples, if you have love for one another" (Jn 13:34-35). Ponder these five words: "As I have loved you." We are to be a community of extravagant love, because we are loved passionately and extravagantly by our heavenly Father. Remember, as we approach the Scripture in lectio divina, we are reading a *love* letter. So, when you open your Bible, open yourself to his love and grace so that you may be filled with his love and in turn extend his love and grace to others and thereby fulfill the law of Christ.

Next, there is our union with God. The practice of Christian contemplation is possible because of the reality of our union with Christ. Nearly 250 times, phrases like "in Christ" and "in him" are used in the New Testament to describe the relationship between the believer and Jesus Christ. Contemplation grows out of this spiritual reality, what John Murray called "the central truth of the whole doctrine of salvation," and this spiritual reality is not something that we achieve through contemplation. Union is a reality established in redemption, but through contemplation this reality can be deepened and experienced as a lived reality.

Our union with Christ reminds us that God is near: "For what other great nation has a god so near to it as the LORD our God is whenever we call to him?" (Deut 4:7). Without minimizing God's transcendent reign, we must also affirm what Paul called the glorious mystery of "Christ in you, the hope of glory" (Col 1:27). This means that we begin our contemplation by confessing that "in him we live and move and have our being" (Acts 17:28). With the realization that we live in God, who is closer than our breath, we direct our prayer toward our individual and corporate heart, where the fullness of God dwells.

God's love for us—and our fundamental union with God, accomplished through the work of Christ—enables us to see contemplation as a place where we can be open before God in love. No need for defenses. No need for explanations or questions. No need even for words. When we get beneath the words and the questions or beneath even our own attempts to appear acceptable (which are unnecessary in light of God's unconditional love for us), it is perfectly natural to rest in the presence of God, aware of our union in love.

Periodically, my wife and I have people come to our property for contemplative retreats, to spend time with God. One of the first questions I hear is, "What should I be doing while I am here?" One answer I supply is, "Oh, nothing.... Just be with God." God's love sets us free to smell the flowers, to explore streams and meadows, to dream or to wonder. In this sense, contemplation is simply the enjoyment of life with our Beloved.

Recent brain studies have shown that as we learn to direct our attention toward thoughts of love and compassion, we actually begin to rewire our brains to make that a more natural tendency. We receive love in contemplation, and through contemplation we learn to honor thoughts and dispositions that foster our love toward others. If *prayer* is the house within which lectio divina dwells, *contemplation*—our resting awareness of the living, loving presence of God with us in silence—is the foundation on which this house is built. When we give place in our devotional reading of Scripture to moments (or seasons) of contemplation, we create a space where our spirit and God's Spirit can simply be present together in the midst of being present with the text of Scripture.

THE PRACTICE OF CONTEMPLATION

Often, in the midst of our devotional reading of Scripture, contemplation simply "happens." We open the Bible and find ourselves needing just to wait for a moment before we read, conscious of the presence that lies underneath the very act of this time of sacred reading. We read or meditate on a passage and find ourselves stopping for a moment, and then waiting even longer, aware of the fact that something is going on between our spirit and the Spirit of Christ. Similarly, we may be drawn to prayer about a passage and then drawn from prayer to contemplation (or drawn from contemplation into prayer). Contemplation has its way of weaving in and around lectio divina.

There are a number of practices that can help calm our minds and make them more amenable to the presence, silence and love that are central to contemplation. First, take a few minutes to do a "brain dump" by recording all the to-dos floating in your head. This will keep them from popping up during your time of contemplation. If other tasks arise, jot them down.

Second, find a neutral spot to return to when you catch yourself daydreaming, distracted or swept up in worries or plans. As mentioned earlier, one ancient strategy is simply to watch your breath. St. Gregory Palamas (1296-1359) suggested that beginners "pay attention to the exhalation and inhalation of their breath, and to restrain it a little, so that while they are watching it the intellect [the wandering mind], too may be held in check." Watching your breath is a subtle reminder that your sitting and breathing is more real than the various imaginations that flit through your mind (remember, the word for Spirit can also be translated *breath*).

Alternatively, prayerfully seek a prayer word or phrase (beloved, Spirit, love, You) that can serve as your anchor. Just repeat this slowly as an expression of your intention of being quiet before God, and return to it as you detect your thoughts wandering. You may switch your prayer anchor from time to time, but keep the same anchor in a given time of prayer.

Third, take note of certain thoughts that appear and seem to take you far afield. Some ancient spiritual writers spoke of a watchfulness of thoughts *(nepsis)*. You learn to recognize the thoughts that are damaging to your time of prayer, and when they first arise, you redirect your thinking by naming this thought ("there's my self-hatred talking again") and then returning to your prayer anchor.

Fourth, get things right with God. Contemplation is essentially about God's presence—or more particularly, a harmonious relationship with God. Underneath the words and the questions is the state of our relationship. If things are wrong in the relationship—however subtle the tensions may be—it will shape what goes on in contemplation. There is a reason why a confession is often placed near the beginning of many Christian liturgies. We need to get things right from the beginning or things will be awkward from that point on (or worse, we are just playing games with God). Your receptivity to contemplation will be greatly enhanced if you pause for a moment at the start of lectio divina, just to check in and remind yourself of who God is and to make things right where needed.

Fifth, use your body. C.S. Lewis aptly reminds us, "The body ought to pray as well as the soul. Body and soul are better for it." Attention to our posture is one way of recruiting our whole person to come before God. There is no best posture for prayer (Scripture approvingly records seven distinct postures), just as there is no best posture for a conversation with a friend. Find a posture that embodies respect, attentiveness and openness. Even a simple adjustment of your hands can help you to be more open and respectful.

And, of course, there is silence and solitude. We have mentioned silence as a dimension of contemplation, but be reminded that silence and its cousin, solitude, are foundational spiritual disciplines in the Bible and are especially valuable for cultivating contemplation. They provide the context for prayer, meditation and fasting. They are like well-prepared garden soil. We can pray anywhere, just as we can scratch the soil and drop in seeds anywhere, but silence and solitude support contemplation like rich and well-watered soil allows a garden to flourish.

We find in Jesus' life a deliberate pattern of seeking out silence and solitude to pray. As Luke recorded, "He would withdraw to deserted places and pray" (Lk 5:16). Similarly, in the preface to the Lord's Prayer, where Jesus mentioned withdrawing from wordiness, he encouraged solitude. "Go into your room," he urged, "and shut the door and pray to your Father who is in secret; and your Father who sees in secret will reward you" (Mt 6:6). Find—or make—those places where you can be alone with God, where you can rest undistracted, where you can be wholly yourself before your Maker.

We open our Bible to read. We the readers interact with both text and Spirit in meditation, using imagination, feelings and more. We hear and speak in prayer. In contemplation, we just sit. God's Spirit is present. The text is still present. We are present. We wait in silence. We are aware of the love between us, between Creator and created. And in this being present, we are made new.

8

ACTING IN THE MIDST OF THE TRIALS OF LIFE

In the martial arts, there is an expression: "mind like water." The phrase describes a person who is ready to respond appropriately to real challenges present. Bruce Lee, the martial arts film star of an earlier generation, urged his listener to let your "mind, be ... like water. Now you put water into a cup, it becomes the cup. You pour water into a bottle and it becomes the bottle.... Now water can flow or creep or drip—or crash!" The message here is that water responds appropriately. When we toss a pebble into a pond, the water responds to the force and mass of the pebble with like measure, just as it would respond appropriately to a large stone. A mind-like-water mindset is open, supple, nonreactive and poised to act appropriately.

This illustrates the mindset we need if we are to respond well to whatever invitation Scripture gives us. We respond appropriately to the pebble-like command to say thank you to a food server; we take seriously the rock-sized call to apologize to our coworker for our ill-timed joke, and we allow the life change from the boulder-like call to alter our priorities so we can care for a family member dying of AIDS.

Acting in the midst of the ordinary trials of life is the last component of lectio divina. Some treatments of lectio divina do not include it, but we (following Hugh of St. Victor, Martin Luther and others) have chosen to close with it. Jesus seemed to think it is important. He warns his followers,

> Everyone then who hears these words of mine and acts on them will be like a wise man who built his house on rock. The rain fell, the floods came, and the winds blew and beat on that house, but it did not fall, because it had been founded on rock. And everyone who hears these words of mine and does not act on them will be like a foolish man who built his house on sand. The rain fell, and the floods came, and the winds blew and beat against that house, and it fell—and great was its fall! (Mt 7:24-27)

Matthew concluded his record of Jesus' Sermon on the Mount with this story. The implication is clear: we *understand* the teachings of Jesus when we *do* them. If reading and meditating and praying and contemplating have no fruit in acting, we have fallen short of Jesus' standard.

Francis of Assisi (1181-1226) was someone who did *not* fall short of the standard. Take, for example, the story of his call to preach. At this point in his life, Francis had met the crucified

Savior and was busy remodeling a church down in the Assisi valley, the Church of St. Mary of the Portiuncula. One day, the Gospel was read, and Francis asked that it be explained. He learned from the explanation that the disciples of Christ should not carry a wallet, shoes or a staff, and that he should preach the kingdom of God (see Lk 10:1-12).

Thomas of Celano, Francis's biographer, wrote that when Francis heard the Scripture and its explanation, he "immediately put off his shoes from his feet, put aside the staff from his hands, was content with one tunic, and exchanged his leather girdle for a small cord.... From then on he began to preach penance to all with great fervor of spirit and joy of mind." Acting on Scripture in the midst of the trials of life. Mind like water, ready to conform to whatever the Scripture might suggest.

SCRIPTURE LEADS US INTO ACTION

The most obvious way to understand the relationship of Scripture to action is that it tells us what to do. As Bible scholar Albrecht Bengel put it, "Scripture teaches its own use, which consists in action." We read the text, discover what it says and then apply it to our lives, determining what actions we need to do in order to obey God's word. And certainly this is a valuable approach, for the Bible *does* tell us what to do in many places (love God, love your neighbor, put away sinful habits and so on).

Nonetheless, a "just do it" approach to Scripture can blind us to the riches of Scripture and its influence on our lives. Scripture is a multidimensional book. It is

- the law (Deut 4:44)
- the sword of the Spirit (Eph 6:17)
- a word of grace (Acts 20:32)
- like fire (Jer 5:14)
- like gold (Ps 19:10)
- like a lamp (Ps 119:105)
- like a mirror (Jas 1:23-25)
- like a scalpel (Heb 4:12)

By its own testimony, God's word is intended to produce

- warning (Ps 19:9-11)
- assurance (1 Jn 5:13)
- blessings (Deut 11:23-28)
- comfort (Ps 119:50-52)
- hope (Ps 119:49)
- spiritual growth (Col 3:16)

Engaged and healthy responses to Scripture will—like water becoming the cup or the bowl—be appropriate but varied: sometimes tears, sometimes laughter, at times deep sorrow and conviction, often a gentle reminder of how things really are.

Another image that might help us fully respond to Scripture is the idea of "receiving" the word. How do you *receive* the word? Let us consider, for example, a comparison. Jeremiah, through his assistant Baruch, delivered the word of God to the king of Judah. In the book of Jeremiah, we hear how the king received the word:

> Now the king was sitting in his winter apartment (it was the ninth month), and there was a fire burning in the brazier before him. As Jehudi read three or four columns, the king would cut them off with a penknife and throw them into the fire in the brazier, until the entire scroll was consumed in the fire that was in the brazier. Yet neither the king, nor any of his servants who heard all these words, was alarmed, nor did they tear their garments. Even when Elnathan and Delaiah and Gemariah urged the king not to burn the scroll, he would not listen to them. (Jer 36:22-25)

The assumption in Jeremiah's story is that hearing the Word of God would have resulted in change. The text suggests that alarm and tearing one's garments would have been a proper response. Yet even when urged to be careful, the king heedlessly continued to burn the scroll.

Now consider the two followers of Jesus on the road to Emmaus. Jesus—unrecognized by them—accompanies the two on their journey. In the course of the trip, he explains the Scripture to them. Then, as Jesus breaks the bread with them, they recognize who he is; and he vanishes. "They said to each other, 'Were not our hearts burning within us while he was opening the scriptures to us?'" (Lk 24:32). In response, they get up and travel back to Jerusalem to tell what they had witnessed.

One burns the text at its hearing. Another's heart burns at the hearing. How do *you* receive the Scripture? Paul praised the Thessalonians; after visiting them, he wrote, "You became imitators of us and of the Lord, for in spite of persecution you received the word with joy inspired by the Holy Spirit" (1 Thess 1:6).

Different passages of Scripture with different people at different points in time lead to different appropriate responses. When you have savored and prayed over a passage of Scripture, often you find that connections naturally arise. Allow your heart to be soft and warm to the text. The response it calls forth from you may be a commitment to change your behavior. But the text may also call forth a response of gratitude or a deeper rootedness of belief. In these cases, simply allow the Spirit to accomplish God's purposes through the text. But there are times when the appropriate response to the text is not clear. One helpful practice is to gently query the text with the questions like the ones we mentioned in chapter five, to see where the connections between it and your life are to be found. Consider asking the following:

- Is there a command to obey?
- Is there a promise to claim?
- Is there a virtue to cultivate?
- Is there an image to savor?
- Is there a warning to heed?
- Is there an example to follow?

The Scripture leads us into action, into response. But as a rich, multidimensional text, it calls forth from us a rich, multidimensional response. Indeed, our understanding of the Scripture and our receiving of the Scripture are inextricably connected. As Douglas Burton-Christie said of the masters of the desert tradition, "Interpretation for the desert fathers always involved the possibility of personal and communal transformation. Holiness in the desert was defined, finally, by how deeply a person allowed himself or herself to be transformed by the words of Scripture."

ACTION DRAWS US INTO SCRIPTURE

Not only does Scripture lead us into action, but our lives draw us into Scripture and draw the Scripture into us. We rightly speak of bringing the truth of the Bible to our lives, but in light of our tendency to self-deception, we need to bring our life to the Bible. What do we find when we ask,

- "What is the word you have for a successful professional?"
- "What is the message for a person going through her fourth round of chemotherapy?"
- "What is the word for me in the midst of constant financial pressure?"
- "What is the word for me in this slum?"

We have to travel in both directions. Reflection to action and action to reflection. We start at the word and bring that to our lives, but also start with our lives and ask what Scripture says to our circumstances. Why do we choose *this* passage to read today? With what "eyes" are we viewing the text today? What do we expect to hear from the text? What life are we bringing to our reading of the Scripture this day? When we allow our lives to bring us into the text (and we are conscious of this movement), we open ourselves in a special way to hear the Spirit through the text.

The Bible is, among other things, a guide for righteous living. Consequently, our reading needs to emphasize both the content of Scripture and concrete life situations. As you think about applying Scripture to your life, it might be helpful to conceive of this as involving (1) the perspective of Scripture and (2) a study of your own life. This model can be viewed schematically as railroad track. The alternating ties represent the study of our own personal experience and the reading.

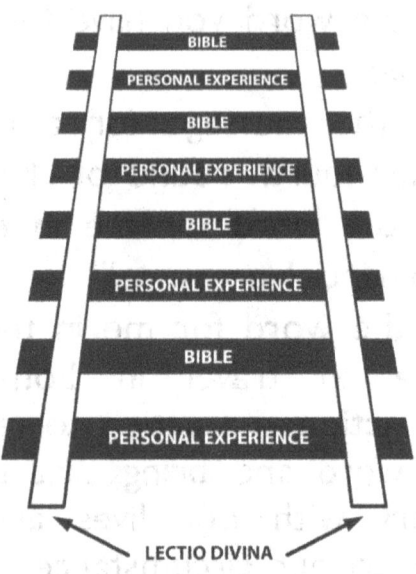

But there is more. Not only does our action/life draw us into Scripture. Our life also draws the Scripture deeper into us. This is Luther's whole point about *tentatio*, or the trials of life. Speaking of Psalm 119, he wrote,

> Thirdly, there is *tentatio*. This is the touchstone which teaches you not only to know and understand, but also to experience how right, how true, how sweet, how lovely, how mighty, how comforting God's Word is, wisdom beyond all wisdom. Thus you see how David, in the Psalm mentioned, complains so often about all kinds of enemies, arrogant princes or tyrants, false spirits and factions, whom he must tolerate because he meditates, that is, because he is occupied with God's Word (as has been said) in all manner of ways.

> For as soon as God's Word takes root and grows in you, the devil will harry you, and will make a real doctor [an expert] of you, and by his assaults will teach you to seek and love God's Word.

Scripture may lead us into action, but it is in the acting—the honest effort to live out the meaning of the text in the midst of the trials of life—that we truly become masters of the word. Remember, this is Luther's formula for becoming a good theologian. In the end, good theology is attained through a life of trying to live the Scriptures in the face of difficulties.

We have now explored a bit of the interaction between text and life in lectio divina. One element leads to another and responds to the others: life, meditation, prayer, reading, back to prayer, exploration of life, contemplation and around again. The lectio divina dance takes us into new steps with God again and again.

But what do we do when the message asks us to do something that is too hard? We must have the courage, with a soft and tender heart, to tell God what we think. We can't hide our divided and confused hearts from God. We can experience remarkable spiritual breakthroughs from times when we admit that what was asked of us was too much.

I can remember hearing words to treat personal enemies with love and to offer forgiveness, and this seemed to be beyond what I could do for the person who came to mind. I admitted the impossibility to God. It seemed as impossible as asking me to lift a thousand-pound weight. It wasn't that I wouldn't—I thought I couldn't. In a tender conversation with God, I decided that I would pray for the person and that, as I was able, I would follow Jesus' invitation to bless her. Pray I did, and eventually I extended forgiveness in a much fuller way. Be honest about where you are in terms of responding. When you can't respond as you sense God's direction, seek a creative alternative, one that begins a process leading to obedience.

There are some dangers about "obedience." As we seek to live out the message of the Bible, the horrors of the twentieth century give us an important reminder of the social evil (the Holocaust, "ethnic cleansings," environmental degradation) that has come through the complicity of those who simply followed orders, who just went with the flow of society, "conform[ing] to the world" (Rom 12:2). This relationship between evil and complicity challenges popular Christian concepts of sin that emphasize the notion of sin as simply individual disobedience and rebellion.

Several studies illustrate the human tendency to conform to authority. Psychologist Philip Zimbardo set up a mock prison at Stanford University in which twenty-four normal college students were randomly assigned to be "prisoners" or "guards." The students quickly began to take on respective roles. The guards, who had been given uniforms and other symbols of authority, quickly moved past their job description and became threatening and sadistic. The prisoners, who had been given ill-fitting clothes and stocking caps, soon took on unscripted roles by exhibiting extreme passivity and viciousness toward out-of-favor prisoners. Due to ethical concerns, the experiment had to be terminated early. The study documented how easy it is for normal people to take on harmful roles when the social situation supports that.

GUILT AND GRACE IN LECTIO DIVINA

What about the guilt feelings that arise as we read? Perhaps you come across a call to care for the poor and you think of how you sneered at the homeless man last week on the way to work. Or you read about the call for sexual purity and cringe with guilt over how you are living. You must be ready to hear the disquieting and challenging word, but you must be vigilant about not giving in to feelings of guilt.

We value friends who can tell us anything—as Proverbs says, "Wounds from a friend can be trusted, but an enemy multiplies kisses" (Prov 27:6 NIV). We accept these words, even when they sting, because we know our friend is unshakably for us. Jesus tells us that the Holy Spirit is for us and will be known as the Comforter, but "when He comes, will convict the world concerning sin" (Jn 16:8 NASB). The conviction of the Holy Spirit may sting, but his work never leaves us feeling dirty, fearing punishment or with a lowered self-worth—those are the result of Satan's work.

Satan's very name means accuser, and that is what he does continually. He is described as the "accuser of our brothers and sisters, who accuses them before our God day and night" (Rev 12:10 NIV). He is relentless in his accusation, not hesitating to get you at a time of weakness. He does this by telling you lies about yourself and using half-truths. Jesus described his deceitful work like this: "When he lies, he speaks his native language, for he is a liar and the father of lies" (Jn 8:44 NIV).

The conviction of the Holy Spirit and the accusation of Satan often begin with the same seed, an awareness of brokenness. The goal of the Holy Spirit's conviction is restoration to the path of flourishing. The end of Satan's accusation is despair, and its telltale sign is a feeling of guilt focused on the past, but the Spirit leads us to think of restoration, repentance and a new future.

Similarly, Stanley Milgram conducted a series of experiments to study obedience and found that a large number (about two-thirds in his various experiments) of ordinary people, in various countries, would administer what they thought was a fatal electric shock to a fellow participant when directed to do so by an authority figure.

These experimental results paint a very clear picture of the human tendency to conform to social expectations. Some of Western civilization's worst crimes (like aspects of the Crusades) were promoted as obedience to Scripture. True, Scripture leads to action, but action should be discerned in the context of the rest of Scripture and a healthy community of faith. We must not think that whatever looks like obedience is necessarily the right action. Remember: appropriate response to Scripture is response to the living God, and godly actions must be conformed (obedient), not to the surrounding culture (which the Scripture condemns as the "world"), but to the character of Christ.

Though we may struggle with the text and with our response to the text, we must remember that the God who is the source of the text is also the source of our life. An African woman from an animist village used to always carry her Bible with her everywhere. "Why always the Bible?" her neighbor asked teasingly. "There are so many other books you could read."

The woman knelt down, held the Bible high above her head and said, "Yes, of course there are many books which I could read. But there is only one book which reads me."

We are "read" by the Scriptures when we receive it into our lives, and when our lives and actions reflect what we hear.

CONCLUSION

We have mostly written of lectio divina as an event—something we do in one sitting on a back porch early in the morning or with a group of friends after a meal together. And yet we can also think of lectio as something that extends throughout our life.

I memorized Psalm 23 as a child, and I have known it by heart for over fifty years. It has certainly become a go-to text when I seek the assurance of God's providential care. When I sit with my Bible on my lap open to Psalm 23, quietly listening to God's assurance of care through the well-crafted and comforting images (contemplation), other ways of having been with the text are there as well. I have read and studied it (lectio), memorized it and meditated on it, and cataloged the images (meditatio). I have prayed through it and written out a structured prayer based on it.

So lectio over a passage can extend over weeks or even years. When we come with a heart ready to hear from Scripture, all those activities of study, meditation, prayer and quiet sitting with the text are available as we wait to hear the word of the Lord.

A prayer is said in Anglican and Episcopal churches "Blessed Lord, who caused all holy Scriptures to be written for our learning: Grant us so to hear them, read, mark, learn, and inwardly digest them, that we may embrace and ever hold fast the blessed hope of everlasting life, which you have given us in our Savior Jesus Christ; who lives and reigns with you and the Holy Spirit, one God, for ever and ever. Amen." This is lectio divina. We come to the Scriptures longing for life, for truth, for transformation. We come to *holy* Scriptures: the word of God, a love letter, a record of human relationship with God. We come prepared to meet the Spirit of God through the text of Scriptures, ready to encounter God through encounter with the text. So we open the Bible. We read, meditate, mark, pray, contemplate, inwardly digest and act. We open the pages of this book with an attitude of openness ourselves; indeed, we come open to *be opened* by God. And as we open the Bible, we embrace and ever hold fast the hope of everlasting life.

I can still remember the street where I detected the feeling for the first time. I was driving past an elementary school in late summer on the way back from my community garden plot with a backseat full of produce. I could not put my finger on what the feeling meant. When I got home, I washed the produce and continued to brood over the feeling. Then it hit me—I wanted to read the Bible! I had read the Bible faithfully for years, but this was the first time I had felt drawn to it.

I sank into a favorite chair, opened the Bible to Deuteronomy, and for the first time that I could recall, I delighted in the simple reading of Scripture. This switch from drudgery and discipline to delight does not always happen, but it symbolizes the big and small changes we have found in our lives and our faith communities through the prayerful reading of Scripture.

We hope that at this point you have caught a vision for the refreshment and life-reorientation that lectio divina can bring. We are not purists who think there is one best way to pull this off. You may want to consider the elements of lectio to be ingredients that you can experiment with in order to concoct the best recipe for you and your situation.

Try reading a small piece of Scripture slowly, attentive to your thoughts in the process. Explore the art of meditation, engaging your mind, imagination and feelings in interaction with a text as you repeat it again and again. Commit yourself to pray before, during, after you read. Pray broken, blessed, receptive, quiet. Allow yourself to experience the presence of God through the text, perhaps in silence or perhaps in the tongues of the Spirit. Allow yourself to love and be loved in the act of reading Scripture. Finally, experiment with *doing* the Scripture. What might it mean for you to live out this or that text in the realities of your life? What might this or that text mean in the midst of the realities of your action? Allow the Bible and your experience to form an ever-developing road of exploration and growth in the Lord.

In recent decades there has been a renewed interest in lectio divina, and we welcome this interest. At its best this growing interest in lectio divina reflects a commitment to trusting Scripture. Often when we speak of trusting the Bible, we think of believing the miracle stories or what it says about creation. That is certainly part of what it means to trust the Bible, yet there is also the level of trusting that the Bible actually is "the Word of life."

In an age of technology—and in an age where the professional is the one who is usually honored—it takes nothing less than an act of faith to believe that the seemingly simple act of reading, praying, meditating on and obeying a mere book can be the path to abundant living. Lectio does require us to believe that Jesus' promise that "I came that they may have life, and have it abundantly" (Jn 10:10) is really true.

When Benedict established monasteries, they were intended to be schools of conversion, learning and sanctification. He saw to it that lectio divina was woven into the daily life. He understood the power of prayerful reading and mediating on Scripture to shape our live direction. What he understood has been shown to be true through the centuries. Men and women who have chosen to read prayerfully and obey the Scriptures have found that "it is not only a book which was once spoken, but a book which is now speaking," according to A.W. Tozer. In it we hear the words of the Master Affirmer calling us to the life our flourishing he yearns to give us.

REFLECTION QUESTIONS AND SUGGESTIONS

CHAPTER 1: THIRSTY FOR GOD

1. The authors begin this chapter by talking about thirst and longing. What are some of your memories of thirst or longing? How have you responded to your own thirsts?
2. Turn to Psalm 1 and slowly read it out loud. Picture the metaphors of the tree and the chaff. What is the difference between the two ways of life pictured in this passage? What would the life of God's people look like if we followed the advice of this psalm?
3. The authors describe lectio divina as a natural process by which sincere Christians devotionally read their Bibles. Why, then, do you think the practice is not more commonly practiced?
4. The authors state in section entitled "THE SWEETNESS AND BITTERNESS OF SCRIPTURE" that "many of us experience an approach-avoidance conflict toward Scripture": we are drawn toward it and concerned by it at the same time. Can you tell a story of your own experience of

Scripture? How have you navigated your own impulses toward and away from Scripture?
5. What is a *formational* reading of Scripture? How do you think this might differ from a merely *informational* reading? How might you develop a personal practice of Bible reading that employs both informational and formational dimensions?

Suggestion: Take one of your favorite passages of Scripture and read it every day for a week. Read it slowly and repeatedly. Don't try to get anything out of it. Just be with it for a week. See what happens.

CHAPTER 2: THE DIVINELY SPOKEN SCRIPTURE

1. How have you *used* the Scriptures in your life—for good or for ill?
2. What are some of the verses or passages of Scripture you have committed to memory? How has that experienced changed you?
3. The authors use the illustration of a love letter to describe Scripture as a personal revelation of God. Have you ever received a love letter? What does it feel like to read

a love letter? What might it be like to read the Bible as a love letter?

4. We speak of the Bible as spoken by God through human words. Do you ever struggle with trying to figure out what is human and what is God in the Bible? How do you deal with this?

5. When have you ever felt *invited* into relationship through a passage of Scripture? What do you think it would take to experience this kind of invitation as a regular part of your personal (or your community's) practice of Scripture reading?

Suggestion: Choose a small book or a few chapters of Scripture, and look up in a study Bible's notes, in a commentary or in some other resource about the historical and social circumstances surrounding the writing of this passage. Now read this portion of Scripture and imagine yourself in the mind of the original writer. What might have been on his mind or heart as he penned these words? After completing the first part of this exercise, take the same passage and think of God, through these human words, as the author of the passage. What do you hear when you read it again from this point of view?

CHAPTER 3: WE WHO LIVE AND READ

1. In section entitled "WE ARE NOT ALONE", the authors present a list of ways that the Holy Spirit communicates to people. Tell something about your own experience of encountering these different ways of the Spirit's work. How have you discovered the Spirit in the midst of the practice of Bible reading? What was that like?
2. How would you describe what you normally bring with you when you open your Bible?
3. How do you know the difference between the thoughts and feelings you bring to your reading and the thoughts and feelings the Spirit stimulates in the course of lectio divina?
4. This chapter uses the illustration of computer maintenance to describe one of the functions of devotional Bible reading. What is your response to this image?

Suggestion: Choose a passage of Scripture to explore, and read it once. Then reflect on what went through your mind as you read it and try to reconstruct what you brought to the text in that reading. Next, read the passage again and then reflect on what the Holy Spirit was bringing to your reading of the text. Try this with different passages and see what you learn about the ways of your mind and of the Spirit's work.

CHAPTER 4: READING

1. What goes on when we read or study any book? What is unique about reading or studying the Bible? What difference does this make for your own practice of Bible reading?
2. Does the more imaginative, intuitive, devotional reading of Scripture text to lead us astray from the clear meaning of the text established through grammatical and historical study? The authors answer a clear "no" to this question. What do you think? Why or why not?
3. How can we give freedom for everyone to read Scripture without opening the church to error? How can we encourage some people to guide others in understanding Scripture, without making Bible reading a practice only for the elite?
4. How do you deal with "tough" passages? How might you deal with them differently after reading this chapter?

   Suggestion: Take a passage of Scripture and read it meditatively, perhaps using some of the suggestions from the section on the practice of reading. Then go back with pen and paper, and describe the process of your reading encounter with God—much as the authors have done in section entitled "WHAT IS READING LIKE?".

CHAPTER 5: MEDITATING

1. Take a moment to reflect on your day, and list those thoughts that most often occupy your mind, those topics on which you naturally meditate.
2. Which of the two word-pictures of meditation (chewing the cud, gnawing a bone) do you identify with the most as you explore meditation? Why?
3. If you were a preacher (or perhaps you are), how would you prepare to present a sermon based on what you have read so far in this book?
4. How do you practice each of the three phases of meditation (slow down, take it in, take it with you)?

Suggestion: Choose a passage of Scripture. Read it a couple of times. Now employ your whole self in meditating on the passage. Try to experiment with using your body, your imagination, your feelings, your inquiring mind. Meditate on this passage with a fresh approach each day for a week. When using these different methods of meditation, what do you discover about experiencing the text anew?

CHAPTER 6: PRAYING

1. What is prayer? What is prayer to *you*?
2. The authors speak of praying *before*, *during* and *after* reading and meditating. How do they understand each of these moments? Which of these is most familiar to you? What might you like to experiment with in the future?
3. How is prayer not merely an act we perform at some point in our practice of lectio divina, but also the "house that lectio inhabits"? What might that mean for our own habits of prayer and reading Scripture?
4. How do you deal with distractions in your devotions? What have you learned from this chapter that might come in handy?

Suggestion: Write for yourself prayers appropriate for the beginning, middle and end of lectio divina. Try them out for a few days in your times of devotion. Then do a practice of lectio for a few days, and after you are finished each time, look back and reflect on your attitude of prayer in general. In what sense was your prayer the house that your lectio inhabited?

CHAPTER 7: CONTEMPLATING

1. Whether or not you thought of them as *contemplation,* what are some recent times when you found yourself "resting in God and enjoying the pleasure of his company"? How have those instances affected your life in general?
2. Tell the history of your experience of God's presence.
3. Some people are used to lots of words and more noise in their relationship with God. Others are more comfortable with silence. Contemplation seems more connected with silence. Why is this the case? Does this mean that noisy people cannot be contemplatives? Why or why not?
4. Why is an awareness of God's selfless, deep and unconditional love vital to the Christian practice of contemplation?

Suggestion: Find a time and place to be alone. Then after reading and spending some time with Scripture, make use of the six suggestions for practicing contemplation presented in section entitled "THE PRACTICE OF CONTEMPLATION". Try this for a full week and see how it affects your devotions.

CHAPTER 8: ACTING IN THE MIDST OF THE TRIALS OF LIFE

1. Describe a time when you felt led by Scripture into action.
2. In what areas of your life are you consciously applying some directive or insight from the Bible? What have been the struggles and results of that action?
3. Why is the "just do it" approach less than optimal when it comes to putting God's Word into practice? What else might be involved in acting on the Scriptures?
4. What have you learned from your reading of this book in general? What do you hope to do differently because of what you have learned?

Suggestion: Now take what you have learned and put it all together. Choose a passage of Scripture, and try spending some time reading, meditating, praying, contemplating and acting (though not necessarily in that order). What about this was helpful?

FOR FURTHER READING

Bickersteth, Edward. *A Scripture Help: Designed to Assist in Reading the Bible Profitably*. Twenty-first edition. London: Seeleys, 1852. Available at http://www.archive.org/details/ascripturehelpd00bickuoft.

Bonhoeffer, Dietrich. *Meditating on the Word*. 2nd ed. Cambridge, MA: Cowley Publications, 1986.

_____. *Psalms: The Prayer Book of the Bible*. Minneapolis, MN: Augsburg Fortress, 1974.

Casey, Michael. *Sacred Reading: The Ancient Art of Lectio Divina*. Ligouri, Mo.: Liguori Publications, 1997.

Franck, Augustus Herman. *A Guide to the Reading and Study of the Holy Scripture*. First American Edition. Translated by William Jaques. Philadelphia: William Hogan, 1823. Available at www.archive.org.

Hall, Thelma. *Too Deep for Words: Rediscovering Lectio Divina*. New York: Paulist Press, 1988.

Howard, Evan B. *Praying the Scriptures: A Field Guide for Your Spiritual Journey.* Downers Grove, Ill.: InterVarsity Press, 1999.

Robert Mulholland. *Shaped by the Word: The Power of Scripture in Spiritual Formation.* Revised. Nashville: Upper Room, 2001.

Magrassi, Mariano. *Praying the Bible: An Introduction to Lectio Divina.* Collegeville, Minn.: Liturgical Press, 1998.

Vest, Norvene. *Gathered in the Word: Praying the Scripture in Small Groups.* Nashville: Upper Room, 1998.

Wink, Walter. *The Bible in Human Transformation: Toward a New Paradigm in Bible Study.* Philadephia: Fortress Press, 2010.

NOTES

CHAPTER 1: THIRSTY FOR GOD

"we may see Christ more clearly": Church Publishing, *Holy Women, Holy Men: Celebrating the Saints* (New York: Church Publishing, 2010), p.305.

"Beneath the surface of everyone's life": Larry Crabb, "Longing for Eden and Sinning on the Way to Heaven," in *Christian Educator's Handbook on Spiritual Formation,* ed. Kenneth Gangel and James Wilhoit (Grand Rapids: Baker, 1997), p.88.

"Sometimes, when I set to thinking about": Blaise Pascal, *Pensées,* trans. A.J. Krailsheimer (New York: Penguin, 1995), p.37.

Jerome (c. 347-420) describing Psalm 1: Jerome, "Commentarioli in Psalmos," in Corpus Christianorum Series Latina, vol.72, ed. Paul de Lagarde, Germain Morin and Marcus Adriaen (Turnhout, Belgium: Brepols, 1959), p.178.

"a methodless method": Thelma Hall, *Too Deep for Words: Rediscovering Lectio Divina* (New York: Paulist Press, 1988), p.9. "the brothers should have specified periods": Timothy Fry, *Rule of Saint Benedict in English* (Collegeville, Minn.: Liturgical Press, 1982), p.69.

"If you study hard in accord with his": Martin Luther, "Preface to the Wittenberg Edition of Luther's German Writings," in *Luther's Work*s, vol.34, ed. J.J. Pelikan, H.C. Oswald and H.T. Lehmann (Philadelphia: Fortress, 1999), p.287.

"who has closely studied these letters": J.B. Phillips, *Letters to Young Churches* (New York: Macmillan, 1951), xii.

formation is a process of trying: See James Wilhoit, *Spiritual Formation as if the Church Mattered* (Grand Rapids: Baker Academic, 2008), and Evan B. Howard, *The Brazos Introduction to Christian Spirituality* (Grand Rapids: Brazos, 2008), pp.267-97.

CHAPTER 2: THE DIVINELY SPOKEN SCRIPTURE

"The Bible claims to contain a message": Thomas Merton, *Opening the Bible* (Collegeville, Minn.: Liturgical Press, 1970), p.17.

And yet we call it *God's Word*: The phrase "word of God" in the Bible refers to the message of God spoken through the prophets, through the apostles, through the Spirit or through the Scriptures. When we, in this book, quote passages that speak of the "word of God" with reference to Scripture, we are doing so with the consciousness that while it is appropriate to infer aspects of the character of sacred Scripture from the Bible's use of "word of God," the passages cited often have a wider reference in mind.

"If the New Testament be a message": Thomas Chalmers, "On the Supreme Authority of Revelation," in *The Works of Thomas Chalmers Volume Fourth: On the Miraculous and Internal Evidences of the Christian Revelation and the Authority of its Records* (New York: Robert Carter, 1840), p.432.

"So willing is he, infinite love": Howard V. Hong and Edna H. Hong, ed. and trans., *Søren Kierkegaard's Journals and Papers* (Bloomington: Indiana University Press, 7 vols., 1967-1978) vol.III, L-R, entry 3099, p.415.

"the Word of God through the words": John R.W. Stott, *Evangelical Truth: A Personal Plea for*

Unity, Integrity and Faithfulness (Downers Grove, Ill.: InterVarsity Press, 2003), p.46.

"it is generally such that one can": Albrecht Bengel, *Bengel's Gnomon of the New Testament: A New Translation*, vol.1, ed. Charlton T. Lewis (Philadelphia: Perkinpine and Higgins, 1862), xxvi.

CHAPTER 3: WE WHO LIVE AND READ

"We were asked to be a person": John Horn, *Mystical Healing: The Psychological and Spiritual Power of the Ignatian Spiritual Exercises* (New York: Crossroad, 1996), pp.20-21.

For example, he notes that Christians: Robert McAfee Brown, *Unexpected News: Reading the Bible with Third World Eyes* (Philadelphia: Westminster Press, 1984), pp.13-14.

"It was as if ... the passage": Athanasius, *The Life of Antony*, trans. Robert C. Gregg (New York: Paulist Press, 1980), p.31. "When he was thinking of those": Ignatius of Loyola, "The Autobiography," no. 8 in George E. Ganss, ed., *Ignatius of Loyola: The Spiritual Exercises and*

Selected Works (New York: Paulist Press, 1991), p.71.

Perhaps the closest equivalent: See Tremper Longman, *Proverbs* (Grand Rapids: Baker Academic, 2006), pp.153-54; Bruce K. Waltke, *The Book of Proverbs: Chapters 1–15* (Grand Rapids: Eerdmans, 2004), pp.91-92; also Timothy Keller, "Preaching to the Heart," address, Gordon-Conwell Theological Seminary, South Hamilton, Mass.

"Everything we do, our every": John Cassian, *Conferences: The Classics of Western Spirituality*, ed. Colm Luibhéid and Eugène Pichery (New York: Paulist Press, 1985), p.4.

CHAPTER 4: READING

"Read some portion of Scripture": Philip Doddridge, *The Rise and Progress of Religion in a Soul* (New York: American Tract Society, n.d.), chap.19, sect. 9; cited from the Christian Classics Ethereal Library edition, p.107. PDF file downloaded from www.ccel.org/ccel/dodderidge/rise.html.

One "hook word," as author: See Jean Leclercq, *The Love of Learning and the Desire for God*, 3rd ed. (New York: Fordham University Press, 1982), pp.73-74.

"First of all the principal points": Philipp Spener, "Spiritual Priesthood," no. 35 in *Pietists: Selected Writings*, ed. Peter C. Erb, CWS (New York: Paulist Press, 1983), p.34. See also Alexander McPherson, *Westminster Confession of Faith*, Complete ed. (Glasgow, U.K.: Free Presbyterian Publications, 1983), p.23.

"We must not fancy": Edward Bickersteth, *A Scripture Help: Designed to Assist in Reading the Bible Profitably* (London: Seeleys, 1852), p.53, italics in original.

"For most people, the understanding": Thomas Merton, *Opening the Bible* (Collegeville, Minn.: Liturgical Press, 1970), p.37.

"In the Scriptures, our eyes": Augustine, "On Christian Doctrine," bk. 2, chap.7, as quoted in Augustus Herman Franck, *A Guide to the Reading and Study of the Holy Scriptures*, trans. William Jaques (Philadelphia: David Hogan, 1823), pp.87-88.

"lest a knowledge of *external* points": Franck, *A Guide to the Reading*, pp.50, 80-81.

CHAPTER 5: MEDITATING

"should meditate, that is not only": Martin Luther, "Preface to the Wittenberg Edition of Luther's German Writings," in *Luther's Works*, vol. 34, ed. J.J. Pelikan, H.C. Oswald and H.T. Lehmann (Philadelphia: Fortress, 1999), p.286.

"Meditation was not, as the word": Douglas Burton-Christie, *The Word in the Desert: Scripture and the Quest for Holiness in Early Christian Monasticism* (New York: Oxford University Press, 1993), p.123.

"He gnawed the bone": Eugene Peterson, *Eat This Book: A Conversation in the Art of Spiritual Reading* (Grand Rapids: Eerdmans, 2005), pp.1-2.

"By memorization, of course": Dallas Willard, *The Great Omission: Reclaiming Jesus's Essential Teachings on Discipleship* (San Francisco: HarperOne, 2006), pp.126-27. See also www.dwillard.org/articles/artview.asp?artID=106#2a.

"We want in any case to rise up": Dietrich Bonhoeffer and David Gracie, *Meditating on the Word* (Cambridge, Mass.: Cowley, 1986), p.32.

"reading and rereading them": Luther, "Preface to the Wittenberg Edition," p.286.

"in typical Dominican writers meditation": Simon Tugwell, "A Dominican Theology of Prayer," in *Dominican Ashram,* vol. 1, no. 3 (September 1982): 134-35.

"Have you realized that most": Martyn Lloyd-Jones, *Spiritual Depression* (Grand Rapids: Eerdmans, 1965), p.20.

There are many other practices: For a survey of various methods of Christian meditation, see Peter Toon, *From Mind to Heart: Christian Meditation Today* (Grand Rapids: Baker, 1987).

Since the early centuries of Christianity: Martin Laird, *Into the Silent Land: A Guide to the Christian Practice of Contemplation* (New York: Oxford University Press, 2006), pp.36-42.

CHAPTER 6: PRAYING

"In the agony of my soul": Phoebe Palmer, "Diary," 1836, cited in *Phoebe Palmer: Selected Writings, Sources of American Spirituality*, ed. Thomas C. Oden (New York: Paulist Press, 1988), p.99.

"speaking, listening, and the space-in-between": Evan B. Howard, *The Brazos Introduction to Christian Spirituality* (Grand Rapids: Brazos, 2008), pp.314-18.

"In the practice of secret devotion": Charles Hambrick-Stowe, *The Practice of Piety: Puritan Devotional Disciplines in Seventeenth-Century New England* (Chapel Hill: University of North Carolina Press, 1982), p.161.

"Firstly, you should know": Martin Luther, "Preface to the Wittenberg Edition of Luther's German Writings" in *Luther's Work s*, vol. 34, ed. J.J. Pelikan, H.C. Oswald and H.T. Lehmann (Philadelphia: Fortress, 1999), p.285.

"All we need to do is read, listen": Mariano Magrassi, *Praying the Bible: An Introduction to Lectio Divina*, trans. Edward Hagman (Collegeville, Minn.: Liturgical Press, 1998), p.113.

"Christians would find no small": Edward Bickersteth, *A Scripture Help: Designed to Assist in Reading the Bible Profitably* (London: Seeleys, 1852), p.41.

We could give many more examples: For other patterns of praying Scripture, see Evan B. Howard, *Praying the Scriptures: A Field Guide for Your Spiritual Journey* (Downers Grove, Ill.: InterVarsity Press, 1999).

"If you pray over the substance": Philip Doddridge, *The Rise and Progress of Religion in a Soul* (New York: American Tract Society, n.d.), chap.19, sect. 9; cited from the Christian Classics Ethereal Library edition, p.107. PDF file downloaded from www.ccel.org/ccel/doddridge/rise.html.

"Further, since the counsel of man": Hugh of St. Victor, *The Didaskalion of Hugh of St. Victor: A Medieval Guide to the Arts*, trans. Jerome Taylor (New York: Columbia University Press, 1991), p.132.

"I seek by reading and meditating": Guigo II, *Ladder of Monks*, trans. Edmund Colledge and James Walsh (Kalamazoo, Mich.: Cistercian, 1979), pp.72-73.

"To pray means to open": Henri J.M. Nouwen, *With Open Hands* (Notre Dame, Ind.: Ave Maria Press, 2006), p.121.

"Listen, my friend!": Ole Hallesby, *Prayer* (Minneapolis: Augsburg, 1994), p.19.

"for our true identity": Leanne Payne, *Restoring the Christian Soul: Overcoming Barrier to Completion in Christ through Healing Prayer* (Grand Rapids: Baker, 1991), p.45.

"Time in solitude may at first": Henri J.M. Nouwen, *Making All Things New: An Invitation to the Spiritual Life* (New York: HarperSanFrancisco, 1981), pp.72-73.

CHAPTER 7: CONTEMPLATING

"Through the grace of the Lord": Gregory the Great, *Homilies on Ezekiel*, cited in Bernard McGinn, *The Growth of Mysticism: Gregory the Great Through the 12th Century* (New York: Crossroad, 1994), p.42.

"heaven has come near": Cotton Mather, *Diary of Cotton Mather*, vol. 1, 1681-1709, ed.

Worthington Chauncey Ford (New York: Frederick Ungar, n.d.), p.278.

The term *contemplation* can be used: Evan B. Howard, *The Brazos Introduction to Christian Spirituality* (Grand Rapids: Brazos, 2008), pp.310, 315-16, 324-25.

"The reflective part, pondering": Thomas Keating, *Open Mind, Open Heart: The Contemplative Dimension of the Gospel* (New York: Contimuum, 1986), p.20.

commonly called "centering prayer": See Jim Wilhoit, "Centering Prayer" in *Life in the Spirit: Spiritual Formation in Theological Perspective*, ed. Jeffrey P. Greenman and George Kalantzis (Downers Grove, Ill.: InterVarsity Press, 2010), pp.180-97.

"I perceived that the silence": Anthony Bloom, *Beginning to Pray* (Mahwah, N.J.: Paulist Press, 1970), pp.92-94.

"we feel a divine energy": John Calvin, *Institutes of the Christian Religion* 1.7.4, trans. Henry Beveridge (Grand Rapids: Eerdmans, 1953), vol. 1, p.73.

"To achieve silence": Kallistos Ware, *The Power of the Name: The Jesus Prayer in Orthodox Spirituality* (Oxford: SLG Press, 1986), p.1.

"the central truth of the whole doctrine": John Murray, *Redemption: Accomplished and Applied* (Grand Rapids: Eerdmans, 1955), p.161.

Recent brain studies: For a readable and comprehensive summary of this research, see Norman Doidge, *The Brain That Changes Itself: Stories of Personal Triumph from the Frontiers of Brain Science* (New York: Penguin, 2007).

"pay attention to the exhalation": G.E.H. Palmer, Philip Sherrard and Kallistos Ware, *The Philokalia*, vol. 4, The Complete Text (New York: Faber and Faber, 1999), p.337.

"The body ought to pray": C.S. Lewis, *Letters to Malcom: Chiefly on Prayer* (New York: Harcourt, 2002), p.17.

CHAPTER 8: ACTING IN THE MIDST OF THE TRIALS OF LIFE

"mind, be ... like water": Bruce Lee and John Little, *The Tao of Gung Fu: A Study in the Way* of *Chinese Martial Art* (North Clarendon, Vt.: Tuttle, 1997), p.138.

"immediately put off his shoes": Thomas of Celano, *The First Life of St. Francis*, chaps. 9-10 in Marion A. Habig, ed., *St. Francis of Assisi, Writings and Early Biographies: English Omnibus of the Sources for the Life of St. Francis* (Chicago: Franciscan Herald Press, 1983), pp.246-47.

"Scripture teaches its own use": Albrecht Bengel, "The Gnomon of the New Testament," 2, in *Pietists: Selected Writings*, ed. Peter C. Erb, CWS (New York: Paulist Press, 1983), p.255.

"Interpretation for the desert fathers": Douglas Burton-Christie, *The Word in the Desert: Scripture and the Quest for Holiness in Early Christian Monasticism* (New York: Oxford University Press, 1993), p.23.

This model can be viewed: The image of the railroad track was suggested by a rail fence model for Christian teaching developed by Ted Ward and can be found in Lois E. LeBar and Jim Plueddemann, *Education That Is Christian* (Colorado Springs: Chariot Victor, 1995), pp.101-2.

"Thirdly, there is *tentatio*": Martin Luther, "Preface to the Wittenberg Edition of Luther's German Writings" in *Luther's Work* s, vol. 34, ed. J.J. Pelikan, H.C. Oswald and H.T. Lehmann (Philadelphia: Fortress, 1999), p.286.

Similarly, Stanley Milgram conducted: These studies are summarized in Stanley Milgram, *Obedience to Authority: An Experimental View* (New York: Harper Perennial Modern Classics, 2009), and Philip Zimbardo, *The Lucifer Effect: Understanding How Good People Turn Evil* (New York: Random House, 2007).

"Yes, of course there are": Hans-Ruedi Weber, *The Book That Reads Me* (Geneva: WCC Publications, 1995), ix.

CONCLUSION

"Blessed Lord, who caused": *The Book of Common Prayer* (New York: The Church Hymnal Corporation, 1979), p.236.

"it is not only a book": A.W. Tozer, *The Pursuit of God* (Radford, Va.: Wilder Publications, 2008), p.54.

BACK COVER MATERIAL

FROM DRUDGERY TO DELIGHT

DO YOU LONG TO DELIGHT IN GOD'S WORD? For many of us, reading Scripture feels more obligatory than exciting, and we don't see many tangible results from our efforts. Yet throughout history, people of faith cannot say enough about the effects of God's Word on their life—how it has renewed their soul, made them wise, brought joy to their heart, given them clarity and perspective, guided their steps, and warned them of danger. Why does our experience of Scripture feel so different?

In this helpful, practical book, authors James Wilhoit and Evan Howard introduce you to *lectio divina*, a way of approaching Scripture that draws you to God by helping you encounter him and hear him speak to you in life-transforming ways. Their simple, easy-to-follow explanation of this ancient practice provides a perfect foundation for you to begin meeting God in his Word as you

READ • MEDITATE • PRAY • CONTEMPLATE

Discover a new experience of God's Word—one that leads you to experience more of God himself.

***

"*Wilhoit and Howard, like trustworthy spiritual directors, invite readers to feast in the house of prayer, in which, they tell us, lectio divina resides ... for all who seek to grow in faith.*"
SUSAN S. PHILLIPS, Ph.D., professor of Christian spirituality, New College Berkeley

"*The authors befriend the Word in such a way that we become better friends of God and more committed members of our faith community.*"
SUSAN MUTO, Ph.D., author of *A Practical Guide to Spiritual Reading*

"*A practical spirituality of the Word, steeped in the tradition of our ancestors.*"
ALBERT HAASE, O.F.M., author of *Coming Home to Your True Self*

***

JAMES C. WILHOIT is professor of Christian education at Wheaton College in Wheaton, Illinois. He is the author of *Spiritual Formation as if the Church Mattered*, coeditor of the *Dictionary of Biblical Imagery* and, with Leland Ryken, author of *Effective Bible Teaching*.

EVAN B. HOWARD is director of the Spirituality Shoppe: An Evangelical Center for the Study of Christian Spirituality, based in Montrose, Colorado. He has served as a pastor and as an adjunct faculty member at Whitworth College. He is also the author of *Praying the Scriptures* and *The Brazos Introduction to Christian Spirituality*.

www.ingramcontent.com/pod-product-compliance
Lightning Source LLC
Chambersburg PA
CBHW011306150426
43191CB00016B/2350